A Name for Every Leaf

A Name for Every Leaf

Selected Poems, 1959-2015

Ashok Vajpeyi

Translated from the Hindi
by Rahul Soni

HARPERPERENNIAL
An Imprint of HarperCollins *Publishers*

HARPERPERENNIAL

First published in India by Harper Perennial 2016
An imprint of HarperCollins *Publishers*
4th Floor, Tower A, Building No. 10, DLF Cyber City,
DLF Phase II, Gurugram, Haryana – 122002
www.harpercollins.co.in

This edition published in India by Harper Perennial 2024

2 4 6 8 10 9 7 5 3 1

P-ISBN: 978-93-5699-719-6
E-ISBN: 978-93-5177-703-8

Typeset in 12/15 Adobe Jenson Pro
By Saanvi Graphics Noida

Printed and bound at
Thomson Press (India) Ltd.

MIX
Paper from
responsible sources
FSC® C010615
FSC
www.fsc.org

This book is produced from independently certified FSC® paper
to ensure responsible forest management.

For Didiya and Kaka

Contents

Preface

The best critics, like the best poets, are shamans. They are capable of leading readers into the inner life of a text – to that dark cavern where its heart pumps and its life blood flows.

While I don't claim to be able to perform that role, and less so when I am reading poetry in translation, I admit I am curious about the heart centre of a book. What fuels the enterprise? Can we feel its pulse? I am curious also about my fellow-poets. What draws them to this stubbornly riddling, twilight language? What do they need to express here that they cannot articulate in the more accessible, daytime tongue of prose?

And so, as a reader, I find myself looking for a line or phrase that unlocks what seems to be the deepest impetus behind the enterprise – the motive behind the crime, as it were.

On reading this volume of new and selected poems by Ashok Vajpeyi, I chanced upon two lines that distilled a recurrent preoccupation: 'As long as you still have words, you can't reach Brahma's forest,' says the poet. But he is quick to add, and not without some wryness, 'This too, we learned through words.'

In one swift stroke you have the paradox central to language – its power and its inadequacy, its capacity to lead us to places of liminality, as well as its inability to penetrate the darkest thickets of human consciousness. In tones that veer from the rueful to the contemplative, the celebratory to the wistful (but seldom despairing), Vajpeyi returns to this theme time and again across his poems.

Poetry with its language of obliquity and shadow is perhaps the only verbal route to at least the outskirts of Brahma's forest. For poetry is essentially a door. 'We forget to close it on purpose' (as the poet says in his essay, 'The Door of Poetry'). Why? Perhaps because we know its business is to be an aperture. It is intended to stay open, to invite wonder and surprise, and to smuggle some of the enchantment from the darker realms into our prosaic, sunlit, everyday worlds.

Vajpeyi's poems play with the idea in multiple ways. On the one hand, there is the capacity of poetry to sustain, to offer perspective ('a window to the infinitude of the world'), to offer connection and wholeness in a fragmented world ('a knock that connects the permanent to presence/... that reminds the inside of the outside'); to awaken and provoke us ('words prod us/like a nail in a shoe'); to offer continuity, legacy, perpetuity ('I want words/the hope that they might live on after me...'); to appease an epicurean appetite for sensual delight and plenitude ('a few words are not enough/to make a poem,/I want all of language'); and above all to offer the age-old talismanic function of sanctuary, protection, guidance ('Words watch over us').

But the poet is also aware that words don't always produce clarity, or beget meaning. When they harden into scripture and ideology, *pravachan* and propaganda, the very same words turn from tools of exploration to weapons of terrifying certainty. This, the poet is aware, is the beginning of the end. It marks the erosion of quest, the annihilation of diversity, the demolition of the tentative, the provisional, the wondering. Once the local is banished, once 'the neighbourhood is cast out of poetry', all we are left with is the steamrolling rhetoric of grand narratives. This is a nightmare world of foam and bluster, a dystopia of abstract nouns and shudderingly impersonal 'universal' truths. There is no room here for the intimate, the uncertain, the homespun. And there is certainly no room for the deep human thirst for personal answers to ultimate questions.

In an essay on the subject, Ashok Vajpeyi once articulated these concerns in persuasive prose: 'Today, the basic struggle of poetry is to protect the personal which the public world is all too eager to devour... Poetry is a civilizational critique of the public from the standpoint of the personal and the individual... It is an unending *satyagraha* against impersonality, totalization and simplification...'

Interestingly, then, this book often reads like a versified defence of the art of poetry. We are reminded time and again of the role that only poetry can perform: its capacity to honour the humble, the paltry, the ordinary, to embrace the overlooked and the marginal, and above all, its capacity to privilege the nuanced question over the jingoistic answer, the uniqueness of the particular over the blurry sweep of the generic. 'Poetry,' as the poet declares, 'does not group things into classes or divisions/It searches for a name for every form'.

Menace is in the air. The poet is aware of it. The fragile ecosystem of art and poetry is under siege. The barbarians – with their tyrannical quest for purity and absolute morality – are never far away. You can hear their battle-cry, the ominous thunder of their hoof-beats. They are almost here, with their love of slogans, their fear of debate, their hatred of contradiction.

And yet, while there is a note of lament at this fast-barbarizing world, the dominant feel of this book remains festive. The mood is spirited, the tone robustly upbeat. Indeed, the poet carves a determined space for 'nowness' and for the first person singular. It is evident in several poems that invoke the work of contemporary artists – musicians, painters and writers. It is evident in the multiple references to the quotidian: the 'weak, watered down tea' and 'the annoyance/of buttonholes smaller than buttons'. And it is evident in a welter of familial and situational detail: 'In Rajpur-Gadheva, Aaji is handing out some … sweets …/and in 44, Gopalganj, Didiya has quickly bathed at the well …/… and in the bungalow at 3-8/74, sunlight glimmers in a corner.'

Location matters. So does the specificity of relationship. And so does the blessed, messy everydayness of life. Indeed, if one were to look for a credo poem, it could well be the one in which the poet champions the right of poetry to enter heaven with 'mud-soaked shoes'.

The Indian preoccupation with community and ancestor endures. The forefathers hover recurrently around these poems. The past may leave us with ambivalent legacies; we may have discovered that our gods are our creations; we may be unable to believe or to pray. But the Hindu joint family stays deeply imprinted in the DNA. The ancestors remain steadfast, offering context and continuity. 'We live,' the poet says, 'in our ancestors' bones.'

The poems also make room – liberal room – for the erotic. Indeed, the poet is playful and exultant as he makes 'a place for love' – sweeping away the stars, pushing aside the sun and moon, and fashioning an unapologetic space for the body, its sensuous possibilities and its mysteries. At no point is the idiosyncratic routed by the ideological; the commonplace devoured by the cosmic; the temporal sacrificed at the altar of the timeless. (Eternity may seem to triumph over time, but eternity and time are also in a relationship of unmistakable reciprocity; one can't do without the other!)

It is not surprising that the poems embrace the carnal and the carnival in a spirit of joyful inclusiveness. 'Carnival' is, in fact, a key word. It is not just in the way in which the poems celebrate 'carne'/flesh, refusing to set up schizophrenic divides between body and spirit. It is also in the way in which they celebrate the deeply invigorating effects of hybridity and plurality. There is no purist desire for a uni-dimensional universe. An older world is not a simpler one. There are no facile nature-culture binaries. Utopia is not an age of a state of noble savagery; cosmopolitanism doesn't mean an absence of rootedness; identity does not spell insularity; the sublime doesn't mean the absence of the sensuous. The barbarians are those who set up dichotomies between tradition and change, the metaphysical and the material, purity and impurity. The civilized are those who know there is no contradiction at all!

And thus, it is in a cheerful inextricable mix of high and low art, the classical and the popular, the global and the local, that Vajpeyi's poetry makes its home. One poem dreams of a land 'where a pundit from Mirzapur would sit in the veranda/And give a sermon on *Ramcharitmanas*/and someone would sit by the light of a lamp/translating Zbigneiw Herbert's poems into Hindi'. There is a longing for a world without rigid hierarchies 'where I could find Shamsher wandering in search of the mot juste/and a school-going child writing a novel in haphazard verse'. There is also a casual blurring of cultural divides as the poet yearns for a world 'where a diner serving kebabs and gosht-do-pyaza Lahore style/could exist next door to Thai fast food joints and Greek bistros'.

There is no hankering after a hallowed past preserved in deep freeze. Refrigeration, the poet suggests, is only for the morgue. 'There must be a geography in which it's possible for all the world's rivers to come together as a carnival...,' he says in one poem. 'The Ganga could borrow from the Amazon some forests untouched by the sun, the Amazon could take from the Ganga some shrines and weathered gods.'

And that brings us to the heart centre, if you will, of Vajpeyi's verse. A verse that returns repeatedly to the notion of confluence. For all the loans, transactions and forgeries, for all the swirling exchange of silt and sunlight, trees and gods, each river is secure, confident of retaining its own uniqueness. The ideal world is one in which old and new, mandarin and demotic, east and west, can coexist. Their relationship is dialogic, sometimes playfully argumentative, but never hostile.

And if anything is privileged in the inspired chaos of this carnival, it is wisdom. The yearning remains for a cosmopolis – perhaps the poet's own version of the mystic poet Ravidas' Begumpura – 'where the city's centre would be a library, grander than any palace'.

It is presumably a library where you would find both Shakespeare and Kalidasa – a library with windows open to the breezes of conversations around the world. A library with a door that never quite closes. It always stays – like the best poems always do – just a little ajar.

Arundhathi Subramaniam

The Beginning

They left
having trampled and destroyed everything
certain that nothing remained intact.
Then, like a worm from a heap of dry leaves
came a word
and taking sand and twigs in its mouth
it began to create.

(2003)

Part I

In Our Ancestors' Bones

We live in our ancestors' bones –

we pick a word
and the syntax of some earlier century
is disturbed,
we open a door
and the sound echoes somewhere in an ancient house –

we live like worms
under the thick cover of plants.

We leave our children
with our ancestors
when we go to work.

We carry in baskets
our burdens and time.
We eat simple food, drink cold water
and walk on
along the road to eternity
gradually fading

out of the scene
so completely that if someone looked
they wouldn't be able to tell
that we ever existed.

We live in our ancestors' bones –

(1986)

Three Songs

For my mother about to give birth

Pieces of Glass

Some pieces of blue glass
and the sun's grace that rains down upon them
you gather them up carefully
because all the eight panes
of your own window are still safe
and the sun's grace
rains down every day
upon your walls too.

Living Waters

You are in love with seasons
and you keep watching for one or the other
in the sky –
like the seasons, your arms are young
and so many of your living waters
circle around you.

But you, there you stand
languorous, with the sun in your face
listening to the babble of a new brook
– with all the green grandeur of a valley.

The Story of Birth

In your eyes are the tiny visions of new eyes,
on your shoulders the slight weight
of new shoulders –
on your lips is the first silence of a new voice
and your fingers possess a new touch
mother, my mother,
how many times you arise from within yourself
and mother, how fresh, how of this very moment
is the story of my birth!

(1960)

When I Return

Mother,
what will I bring
when I return?
The weariness of my travels,
a suitcase full of clothes for everyone,
sweetmeats, toys,
sandals of the latest fashion
                    for my grown-up sisters?
Or some fresh alchemy of blood
and tall tales of valour?

Will I return and say
I have spent my days – like a rich man
watching the unblemished morning
move upon mossy building walls
from the window of my curtained room?

Or fighting the sea single-handed
from desert islands
in defence of trivialities?

Will I tell you
that I have come
from sunless caves

where starving lines
shout out every now and then
amidst shrieks of vultures and hawks
your favourite song, mother
'Raghupati Raghav Raja Ram…'?

Should I say
rejoice, mother, the end has come
– which you'd been waiting for
because I have witnessed
a fearsome incarnation arrive
astride a blue horse?

Or will I only be able to tell the story
of the death of a man with a sunken impotent face
riding a blue horse
in a tiny village?

Or will I, avoiding your sharp gaze
give my little brother
along with other toys
a blue horseman made of wood?

– Will I return
with my arid eyes filled with humiliation
that now covers every road

like the sky,
and then
will you see for the first time
your own god-afflicted face
hidden in mine?

Mother,
what will I bring
when I return?

(1964)

Father's Shoes

There's a paternal tree
near some crumbling terrace of the blue infinite
outspread but rootless,
and under it those black shoes
of dead leather,
slightly splayed from the pressure of feet that once lived
and live no more.

The feet live no more
nor does the man
who kept them in that corner
and quietly went away
to sit on some other terrace and make
plans for the journey ahead.

The colourful birds hopping on the tree
overshadow
those empty shoes
but the colourless tree throws
the shadow of a thin branch upon them
not to protect them from the sun
but to subtly let them know

that it remembers their presence.
The shoes, even if they try, can't remember
the feet that used to wear them.

They dream of tiny feet
for whom they'll always prove too big.

(1978)

The Earth Rescued from Parrots

Our house lies on the route
the parrots take
to go to the jungle
and to come back from there.

Green lines of countless parrots
go to and fro in the sky above us
and a few of them
even stop to rest on our trees.
We live in the city,
how could we know
from what jungle to what forest
from what daybreak to what workplace
the parrots go every day –

often my daughter and I
place bets
on which flock of parrots
will stop or not stop on our trees.

The parrots don't see us
because their sights are always
trained on the trees and their fruit.

The parrots
turn into a green sky
and cover the earth.
The parrots leave the earth behind
like half-eaten fruit.

My daughter
chases after the parrots,
to save the fruit,
the earth.

In the sky, in the dark
the parrots vanish into the distance.

My daughter is left standing
shining with green
caressing the earth, comforting it.

(1985)

A Song to Welcome My Newborn Grandson

1.

In Delhi, before the fog descended
when our anxious eager vigil through the twilight
had left us exhausted, though now the sun was out in
the winter morn,
that's when he came
when I thought *she* would come!
The sound of crying in the coarse and filthy world of
the noisy hospital
as if god had softly called and
opened his door once again:
a star said, let me go play once again
in the heat and dust of earth,
in the mud of time,
in the clay of being and nonbeing.
My younger brother Rajjan said
Why don't you ask, perhaps it's Didiya or Kaka who
has come back?
It was hard to imagine that gods and ancestors were
hovering about
but certainly, the bright and colourful flowers of their
blessings were in the air.

Then a cry, then a squeal, then a footstep,
then a word, then a name, then a number,
then an auspicious beginning.
The greatest wonder in the world
encircling both sky and time
holding all glories in a tiny fist
in a homely bundle
of worn clothes –
another straw in a bale of hay,
another word in the universe of poetry,
another hand to make an offering of wood to the
sacrificial fire.

2.

We had prepared for him;
had arranged a room and clothes and other things;
but what we had was a sheet full of stains,
a grimy, crumpled world,
a house full of right and wrong and a thousand other
pieces of junk,
a crowded, stinking government hospital,
an old but stubborn and chaotic life.
Still amidst all of this
there was the possibility, there was the space for a birth.

Trees must have quivered,
plants must have become restive and
the sap must have quickened in their veins,
birds must have made a nest somewhere out of straws
and scrap,
words, roused out of their silence, must have called,
in the toyshop a bear must have shoved a dog aside to
see who's coming –
gods must have added some more ghee to their votive
lamps so that the flames would burn bright and steady:
an age-old ancestor must have told the others to sit
straight so that she could see clearly
and say whom he'd taken after.

Going is perpetual
and so is coming;
perhaps the one who was going
didn't even know that he's coming too.
But when *he* came
all going ceased for a moment
and it was as if in that interval
we had become immortal.

3.

What is this that has joined us?
What is this that we didn't even know of
but is now ours, one of us,
the one we hover around?
Who is this that when he smiles in his sleep
the entire house blooms like a flower?
Whose cries are these
that in the cool dark of midnight
sound as if
a star is weeping in the sky?

What is this, like a god in a temple,
that the day can't begin without seeing him;
that the afternoons can't pass without petting him;
that the night can't begin without seeing
him smile in his godlike sleep;
that nothing in the house can gleam without the glimmer
in his eyes?

Even those who used to sleep soundly now wake up
many times each night
sometimes from the sound of crying and sometimes just
from worry
and tiptoe to his room to see whether
he's asleep or crying –

he's changed time in the house, changed the seasons:
it's only morning once he wakes up,
lunchtime is in the evening and
dinner a little before midnight.

All night they take turns to visit him
his invisible ancestors
all sorts of gods,
the world has turned into a warm cave and settled in
his room.

It feels as if the dewdrops falling outside
are the tears of an infant god.

4.

In Rajapur-Garheva, Aaji is handing out some stale-
looking sweets from her store to everyone;
and in 44 Gopalganj, Didiya has quickly bathed at the
well and is preparing sweet fritters;
Amma's complaining that the auspicious hour has come
but no one has prepared the lamps for prayer;
at T-14 Mukherji Court St. Stephens, someone has
entered the room before I could;
and in the bungalow at D-8/74 sunlight glimmers in
a corner:

Everyone is coming
swimming through the air, invisible
wrapped up in time,
surrounded by death, they're all coming –
they've circled around the brightly shining line
which the faltering footsteps
he had arrived on made
but which isn't yet a trail;
like a freshly-washed lamp still redolent of sand
like a star that shines until late in the morning
like a word from outside the dictionary that's come into
a poem
like sunlight like moonlight like dew
like light like colour
like an unwritten letter of the alphabet –

I see again with my ageing eyes that
everything is perpetual –
that life is unbroken
that we don't die or pass away
that we go on being again and again
yet always as if for the first time
and this time truly as if for the first time.

(1999)

A Prayer for My Grandson on His Second Birthday

Despite turning sixty I still don't
remember all the words to a single prayer:
I never saw my father praying,
my mother never taught me one.
I have lost many things
but not prayer,
because I never really had any.

You are a lisped sentence
around which I want to weave a prayer:
I want the warmth of sunlight, the diffidence of green leaves,
the unflagging zeal of birds,
the magical aura of toys,
the sound of grain in a pot,
a sleep heavy with dreams,
stars lost in the sky,
helping hands, comforting eyes and tireless feet
to be its warp and weft.

For you I wish not freedom from fear but irrepressibility,
I don't want you to get anything as a gift or a boon.
I know that as you grow up the world
will be as mixed-up and murky

as it will be for me while I grow old:
but I can give you no flame to fight the darkness,
nor any cane to feel your way through.
I can only wish that
sooner or later you find your own fire, with its own life
and light
which you will fight for and somehow keep burning
until the end.
I always found it hard to differentiate between dream
and reality,
perhaps you will be able to tell them apart early in life –
but I still want
the thread that guides you from the beginning to the end
to be made of dreams, even if intertwined with truth:
we belong to the family of dreams, not the clan of reality.

It's not a dilemma but my responsibility
to bequeath ancestors to you instead of gods:
to tell you that we may have had our losses
but without surrender, without regret;
that we may have been indebted
but we always walked our own path;
that we have made ourselves useful in times of need
even if we were forgotten afterwards.

Our time will turn out to be no better or worse than
yours:
it, too, overflows

with love, with desire and greed,
with injustice and rage, with hatred and anxiety,
but it also contains radiant mornings and sad assurances,
long nights without end, nameless birds,
trustworthy words, moments that will persist until the
end of time,
old people active until their last, structures that collapse
and overturn,
architectures of hope, soaring aspirations,
and dusty but indelible truths.

What you will take from these as your inheritance is
up to you
but we will remain around you invisible like time,
like grace,
which might keep you from losing your light in any
situation.

My grandson,
you who are without deceit like god,
spontaneous like the universe,
newborn like the sun,
holy like fire,
ancient like the earth,
with these words I greet you
and hope
that these words form a prayer.

(2001)

Lament

I regret:
that I couldn't make a home
where Didiya-Kaka, Amma-Dada, Baba could live
with Ribhu,
which contained at least one century, if not centuries
wide and open like a veranda;
in which everyone would gather to eat
under the kathchandan and bakauli trees;
where there would be ice-cream and langra mangoes
with jackfruit pickle, lentil fritters and stuffed bitter
gourd,
where there would be matar-paneer and chole with
naan;
where a pundit from Mirzapur would sit in the veranda
and give a sermon on the *Ramcharitmanas*
and someone would sit by the light of a lamp
translating Zbigniew Herbert's poems into Hindi;
where the heavy wooden doors would remain open
from five in the morning to eleven at night
with no one standing guard;
where I'd sit in a corner
and listen to Anandmohan Dada
reminisce about Nirala and Ramchandra Shukla.

I regret:
that I could not live in a neighbourhood

where you could find men, women and children from
centuries new and old
strolling in the park at the break of dawn;
where there would be a provision store, Mahadevi
Mithiya's sweetmeats,
a tea stall, a milk bar, an ice-cream shop;
and a tailor repairing garments from the twelfth century;
a grocer washing and laying out fresh vegetables from
the twenty-third century;
where I could find Shamsher wandering in search of
the mot juste
and a school-going child writing a novel in haphazard
verse
with no regard for grammar;
where Junu's car wouldn't want to pull ahead of
old man Daua's oxcart going towards the fields.

I regret:
that I could not find a city
with walls to keep the barbarians out,
where rows of colourful flowers
would appear like gifts,
where merchants in the bazaar would sell embroidery
from Baghdad
to soldiers from America;
where a diner serving kebabs and gosht-do-pyaaza
Lahore style

could exist next door to Thai fast-food joints and Greek
bistros
and shops selling herbs and spices from Turkey;
where the city's centre would be a library, grander than
any palace
where at the touch of a button you could read
lines from Kabir and Shakespeare
in infinite languages.

I lament
only in poetry
because there's no other space left
for regrets or dreams.

(2003)

To My Father

Now when nothing remains between us
except some sadness and regret
and we've forgotten
your anger, your failures
your apprehensions about me,
we can see that
while prestige may be easy to come by
dignity in life only comes with great difficulty.
Life is a miser with dignity
and we've both had delusions of possessing it.

We were able to forget
no insult, whether from gods or devils,
even though such forgetting is natural, even necessary
to get through the struggles of life.
Why did we find
insult more memorable than failure,
perhaps it is a familial failing,
the self-respect of a farmer's son,
the self-deception of a small-town poet.
It's thirty-five years since you left
and I am older now
than you were then.

You never had the time to understand me
and I was always trying to test you:
now when nothing remains between us except some
sadness and regret,
if you saw how weary I am you'd feel
that in my wilfulness, in my unwillingness to let an
insult pass
I have only emulated you:
the truly sad thing is not
that so many years passed in misunderstanding
but that
in the end I've turned out to be a pale imitation of you
which neither you nor I
ever suspected
or desired.

(2007)

Part II

Ali Akbar Khan Plays the Sarod 1

Where every now and then a yellow rose crashes against
 the window
there she stands, hunched and crying
and I listen...
    someone keeps pulling
    the trembling black sky
    towards me,
    keeps on pulling –

(1959)

Ali Akbar Khan Plays the Sarod 2

On the radio, on a dull spring night

A timid hand
lay frozen upon the banister

(Epilogue written after the playing stopped)

The light of spring
yellow, slow
and blossoming and trembling in it
a golden sky of rocks and flowers:
I turned around and looked –
she
was behind me
but dissolved suddenly
into shadows –
and the festival of day
ended right there,
its fog, its morning, its sunlight
and its green lines of parrots.

A timid hand
lay upon the banister
a soft flow of light
gushed forth from the fingers –
a timid hand

(1959)

On Suddenly Remembering a Painting by Husain

Two deep red eyes of light
are trained upon the road
that passes close to the darkness
of my home.
In the fog that sleeps upon the lake
        someone laughs
        a giggling grey laughter.
Over the tops of the dark lines of trees
        someone laughs.
The sky become overcast – black
        – my home, released from the deep red eyes
emerges and sinks
in the darkness, on the road,
endlessly in the dim yellow light...

(1959)

Still Bird, Flying Stone

For the painter Jagdish Swaminathan

The stone wants
to be able to fly
like the bird
in the sky
to be able to see the world beyond the valley
to be able to touch it and return.

But the bird doesn't want
to trade places with the stone
to be still like it for centuries
to be able to see only
the blue sky and other stones.

Yet
the bird is still, like the stone.

And like the bird, the stone takes flight.

There on the stone
sitting, not sitting
a bird that flies,
a bird that's still.

(1979)

Mallikarjun Mansur

Setting his own pace
Mallikarjun Mansur
comes in
late
and marches ahead of time

ahead of a time
that's filled with confusions, riddled with wounds
that's growing more and more inconsequential,
a time that trails him
grovelling
destitute and crippled
begging for alms with outspread hands –
panting

Mallikarjun Mansur
advanced in years but standing tall
leans over
death
keeps a hand on its shoulder
stops and lights a beedi
then starts walking once more towards some new
destination

his saintly hands take nothing for themselves
they only give wherever they go
and so he sings his way through the wide world
if god
came this way
he would not be able
to tell himself from Mallikarjun Mansur

(1992)

Being Earth, Nonbeing Sky

From a requiem for Kumar Gandharva

The grass growing on the ruin's walls
is a green sign from the earth
that it's time
to return to dust.
Being has a time
has colour
has turns and descents
nonbeing is timeless, colourless.
Time
sitting on a branch of a tree in some garden
nibbles away like a parrot
at being –
in nonbeing, there's not even a footprint of time.
Time knocks
on the door of a house
where no one lives.
Time stands with its begging bowl
outside that door
from which no one will emerge.
There is no time now
no provisions for the journey
no tired feet
no sweat on the brow.

The steps leading to the temple
the final cries of sacrificial animals
the bloody end
of goat song.
In the sunlit darkness of blood
the scream of stone
the call of grass
the cries of greenery.
Being
earth
nonbeing
sky.

(1992)

No Time for Leave-Taking

From a requiem for Kumar Gandharva

What images, what colours
what time
does leave-taking choose?
Rocks, steady in their deadened light
mountain ranges that hold fast the drowning day
silence held back, like the desire to sing in the dark
greenery shining forth unimpeded from plants
a plate, after dinner, dotted with leftovers
a bucket brimming with lukewarm water
a hand raised to fasten a chain
the profound silence of sleep's hushed dreamless valley
the semi-wakeful state before the birds begin to chatter
... who can say when, suddenly
someone might say
farewell?

Farewell
to incompleteness
to buds and breasts and lovemaking
to word-meanings and silence and metaphors
to song and patience and unborn grandchildren
to the corporeal and the incorporeal
to the man on the dark deserted street in the morning
to the woman grinding spices while wiping away tears

to the duplicity of gods and to their quarrels
to the alphabet
to starting letters and half-formed sentences
to was and is and will be
to every pronoun
to clusters of verbs and whirlpools and windows and
glass
to the sunlight of squirrels and the leisure of birds
there is no time for leave-taking
every moment is a farewell
whatever takes place
takes its leave
often without even realising it.

(1992)

Raza's Time

A poem for the painter Syed Haider Raza on his eightieth birthday

1.

I pick names
from the forests of Madhya Pradesh
Kakaiya, Babaria, Bachai, Mandla, Damoh, Narsinghpur
and they twinkle and glimmer in your sky
like dew-drenched plants –
like glowing letters from the alphabet of your primal
soul:
I cannot hear
the hiss of a snake entering a crack in the house from
the jungle of your childhood,
or the sting of a scorpion crawling in the veranda,
but the tables being recited in the village school porch
and the religious verses of Tulsi, Kabir, Rahim
being repeated from a slim Hindi textbook
wash over me like prayer.
Fear and beauty live together in the forest
and fireflies flicker now and then in the intimate
darknesses of home.
Is it a fog spreading through the forest or
the smoke from burning leaves

that you pass through with a forest guard
on the way to Mandlato see the Mahatma
address a public gathering –
and years later the memory of it will stop you
from going to the other side after Partition
unlike your brothers and your first wife.
Your strict, honest father
teaches you the power of namaz five times a day,
and from the neighbouring Hanuman temple you hear
recitations of the *Ramcharitmanas*,
and you bow your head in prayer in a church in Paris:
who knew, maybe not even you, that one day
colours and shapes would form the silent words of your
prayer,
that the chirping of birds in the forest, the roar of a
panther that ever so often struck
fear into the hearts of villagers
and the sound of a river in spate in the dark of night
would all combine to form a prayer
giving you the boon
of creating
of searching and finding,
of being of aid to others
wherever you may be.
A boon that no one knew about
but which always contained the warmth of the soul
and its incomprehensible fear too.
When you call upon divine powers

this is the boon that showers invisibly
the way jasmine flowers shower every morning after
the rains
turning the circle underneath a little white, a little
orange, and fragrant for a little while.
We get back only what we have given
even if it was long ago and to someone whom we don't
even remember.

2.

The colour of stone changes very slowly –
often you don't even notice when the colour of a face
has changed –
despite burrowing deep underground the dark roots,
too, have a colour –
even when they reach the surface aquatic plants still
shimmer in their own colours –
a note only shines through in a raga
when a singer colours it with his own private pain:
Does a forgotten colour from childhood return in old
age?
Does the colour of youth glow again in some nightmare?
Does the colour of love,
of solitude,
of desire and longing

survive under the light and shade of the canopy of years?
In the dark the colour on the canvas
softly whispers
to the colour in some tube on the floor –
one colour crawls to the easel before fading away,
one colour knocks at the door to the invisible,
one colour, walking slowly, steadily upon a line reaches
a circle,
one colour advances, trembling like a leaf,
one colour, like a word, becomes restless in its place,
one colour burns out without ever lighting up,
in this battle of colours,
in this wilderness of colours,
agitated by colours, at peace among colours,
you stand
a colour-burnt man –
pure and bright and tender
and in the light of my words I see
that the earth for once is changing colour
as if it is the sky,
as if it is the wind,
as if it is fire or water.

3.

The prehistoric stone you keep in your studio
lies silently in history.
The wooden statue of a woman
hanging on your wall
stares at you every day from across centuries
as you kneel and paint
or whisper lines
from Rilke's poems to yourself.
It's as if the Narmada's uninterrupted time
flows to touch your fingers each day
and finds tranquility:
the vital French time of Paris
breaks the bounds of pain, compassion and revolution
and falls upon your window like sunlight sometimes
sometimes like fog and mist
sometimes like darkness.
You, unperturbed but restless,
silent but intense,
old but bent,
have kept on searching for
seeds, germination, efflorescence, trees,
leaves, triangles, points, rays.
Time picks,

without your seeing or knowing,
from your own collection
a statue of Ganesh and anammonite relic,
a prayer, a passage from an ancient Jain manuscript,
a page of verses from the Quran,
and reads them like a complete text
as if hidden within it is the secret of you being
who you are
beyond your age, your colours, and your time.

4.

Time isn't childhood:
while it can be adorned with toys
seeds, rocks, threads and scraps
it can't preserve them, or even remember them.

Time isn't the veranda of a primary school's rustic
building:
in which your teacher drew
a point on the wall
and told you to focus on it forgetting everything else –
you touch that faraway point again and again
and from your touch originates the whole world.

Time isn't a window that looks out upon a road:
you open it now and then
to let the sun come in
or to gauge the wind and cold outside –
but nothing else appears from it in your colours and
shapes.

Time isn't a stone building surrounded by trees and
shrubs:
sometimes you lay out paper on the heavy stone table
inside,
sometimes your desires,
sometimes all the sadness you have collected in your life,
but you can't live in them
because you live in indelible colours,
in their luminosities,
in the darknesses pulsing between their layers.

Time that transforms,
that makes and breaks as it pleases,
that calls out and sings,
that gasps and flutters
you remain unaffected by it
as if time doesn't even exist for you,
and although lines of poetry emerge from your
paintings –
there's no place for time in their structure.

Time is not the staircase in the sixteenth century
building at Cité du Couvent
made to fetch supplies from the neighbouring market.
Time is the silence that lives in the veranda in front of
your home,
time is a thin hair that has broken off your brush,
time is the expectation of mystery in your eyes,
time is the vibration of flesh:
without any fuss
you go outside of time.
Time is the cloth that has been used many times to wipe
paint-stained hands.
Time is the statue of Nandi lying on the edge of Lake
Futera in Damoh
which looks at you unblinking even today
as if you are an ineffaceable point.

5.

On a trail in the forest
by the side of a stone-paved road
far away, from a window in some tall building
in some half-forgotten line of a poem
in the agitated wilderness of shapes
colours giggle like children

and slowly turn into tears, into dew,
into the heated waters of desire:
a line is drawn across time
burning, incandescent like fire.
The world stops,
lit in its own colourful aura
it pauses for a moment on the verge of beauty.

6.

Did colours ever know that prayer lived in them?
Did geometry ever feel that it possessed the structure
of prayer?
Did a painting ever realise that it was a page from a
prayer book?
Even if you're not kneeling,
even if your head isn't bowed in humility,
even if your fingers are tangling with colours
having forgotten everything else,
you are always in prayer
because for you the whole world
is a never-ending prayer,
to which, with great apprehension,
you're adding a few new words.

7.

In the soul's heat
desires still exist despite turning to ashes –
words still exist despite being used up in paintings –
the heart's call still exists despite having vanished in
prayer –
we consecrate
with what is left
with what will persist beyond time
despite the attempts of death –
with hands wounded by time
we consecrate
him who is outside of time.

(2001)

An Elegy for Kamlesh

Perhaps there was a knock on the door this morning
and you opened it and went away:
it's hard to say
if it was in the light or in the dark –
who knows, perhaps life is the only possible light
and everything else some kind of darkness.
You didn't take leave from anyone before you left:
not from your poems and books,
not from your surroundings that you had tended with such care,
not even from life perhaps –
you just went.
We came with you to the village's edge
but when we reached it
you didn't turn back, and went on ahead.
Before us all is the life that remains
and death is behind us –
all we are is a meal for death
sitting in the lap of life.

The world goes on as before –
the earth moves on its path round the sun,
the sky controls its planets, stars and galaxies,
the weather's unbearably hot and humid,
people run to and fro

busy with work –
suddenly you're not amidst this,
a leaf falls, a star breaks,
a word stops,
a hand slips out of a hand,
water dries up in a pot,
a handful of grain falls to the ground,
a lamp goes out after burning all night.
The world goes on as before.

Who can say whether the ancestors know
that you have come into their shade?
Whether the gods have got the news
that you, who had forever been searching
for the essence of their being, have come?
Whether the many deceased words realise
that the one who had given them new life
has himself passed away?

Who wants to be here –
in this world that we have been ruining,
where hope for light is ever-diminishing,
the love of which won't save us from disappearing in
the end?

Do we only do all that we do
to kill time
to evade death just a little longer
before returning to the invisible?

Is the meaning and mystery of our nonbeing
bound up with our being?
Is being just a small interval
between nonbeing and nonbeing?

There in the other world
the gods won't need books
even though they're fond of scripture –
time won't exist
nor space for poetry in the unending infinite.
When there'll be no distance between the body and
the soul
how will there be occasion for any art?
How are we to even know whether
the sights and smells of this world ever reach there?

Can there be
light without a lamp, a home without walls,
prayer without words, sight without eyes,
can we be there without being?
Or will we be an entry, a number in some ledger?
Or not even that?
When we won't be here
then how and why will we be there?

If we have to burn and turn into ashes,
if mortality has its grip on every moment of our lives,
if we can take nothing with us,

if our desires have to turn to dust,
if in our beginning is our end,
then why do we live, why do we try so hard?
Why do we think
that we will survive in some way after we end?

We sully everything
because we're human – truth, honesty, virtue,
good wishes and good fortune too:
we cannot keep the sheet spotless
because we are human:
even our purity is, in some way, sullied.

Sooner or later there'll be a knock on the door,
there'll be a call for us
and we're ready, though we don't await it:
there's neither the time nor the will to break free from
worldly desires now:
poetry after all is the science of worldly desire.

(2015)

Part III

No Beginning, No End

There was once a No-Beginning, there was once a No-End. No-Beginning didn't like being in the beginning, and No-End didn't like being in the end. But if there was no beginning there could be no end. The matter of the middle was more complex: because if there was no beginning and there was no end, then where could the middle be? They all wanted to be, but couldn't decide where. It occurred to No-Beginning, that having no end was the same as having no beginning. No-End, on the other hand, felt that having no beginning was the same as having no end. Each one felt that the other was unnecessary. But neither one could exist without the other. This wasn't just a game of logic. The middle meanwhile lay neglected: the other two couldn't be bothered about it. One day No-Beginning and No-End got bored and decided to play a game, pretending to be a train: they got behind one another and started going round in circles. And ever since, they've been playing, No-End behind No-Beginning behind No-End behind No-Beginning behind No-End behind No-Beginning, to forget the ennui of having no place.

(1990)

Behind, Ahead

Someone was following me. Or at least that's what it felt like. The important thing was the feeling, not the following. If you see or if you feel that someone is ahead of you, it doesn't make you afraid. But if it's behind, then it does. Even if you don't know who's ahead, what he's like or why he's there, it's still reassuring when someone is up ahead, and it seems unlikely that he'll turn around and attack. And even if he does, there will be enough time to see him turning, to brace for the attack and to prepare to counter it. But whoever is behind is not to be trusted. Perhaps he's only following in order to attack you. If he suddenly does something, then you'll have no time to prepare yourself for it. You expect the one ahead to know the way, to be familiar with its dangers. And this precisely is the scary thing, that the one behind has expectations from the one ahead, whereas the one ahead fears the one behind. Hope and fear, fear and hope. And that's how the way passes by, whether or not you reach anywhere.

(2005)

Words on the Wall

Something was written on the wall. Was it a slogan, a mantra or a curse? What difference does it make? Because they were just words after all. Not a message for someone in particular, but for everyone. But not all passers-by would read them. Not even the peanut-seller who sat against that very wall. The wall with the fading words, the people passing by unaware, and sitting comfortably right under them, the peanut-seller. But to words used to living in scriptures, inscriptions, books and newspapers, this didn't seem odd. They were used to being thrown into or written on any blank space. They were letters. Fading letters. They didn't contain meaning inside them, the way peanut shells contain peanuts. If you burst or break them, meaning doesn't come out, just more words. And that was the most beautiful and terrible thing about the writing on the wall, that the meaning of words was even more words. And still is.

(1990)

No

We had no knowledge of what to do or where to go. We had no time to think even. No, there was time but we had no inclination. No, there was inclination but we had no courage. No one wants to go to a place when they don't even know where it is. No-where gives rise to fear. No-thing too. Often even just No. That's why we set off with no preparation. No, there was a little preparation. We had no hope of getting anything. We had no reassurance of getting anywhere. We had no belief that there even existed somewhere that we had to reach or something that we had to acquire. It was hard to walk in the middle of, or surrounded by, so much No, but we had no choice. There was indecision, there was confusion, there was guilt, there was also repentance, but there was no choice. This too was another No. To keep on walking was either obstinacy or compulsion. We could have not walked. But far away there was a flash, a flicker – there was the possibility of sudden illumination. It was there and it was also not there. It was a difficult situation. In the gloaming, in the dusk, there was a trail that no one had taken before. We thought that if we took it, no one would see us. It was the trail of No. The path of No, the street of No. The road of No. We had walked so far but had ended up at No after all.

(1990)

Brahmaranya

It was at the very end. Words had been left behind, touch had been lost. Beauty had gone into hiding and taste had disappeared. Not even smell remained. We had reached that forest in search of ways to get lost: it was Brahma's forest. Brahma's jungle, Brahma's wilderness. There was wind, but the skin couldn't feel it. There was light, but the eyes couldn't see it. Darkness, rays of light, clouds, rain and stars, they were all there, but the sky could not be seen. And that sky had its own sky. The great sky. It was at the very end: forest and sky. We had reached there alone. But if we are able to turn that memory into words, then we hadn't really reached there at all. Leaving everything behind, losing everything, holding on to only words, we didn't know where we had reached. It wasn't Brahma's forest. As long as you still have words, you can't reach Brahma's forest. This, too, we learned through words. But as long as there are words, can there be Brahma, can there be a forest?

(1990)

Shubhsrava

There's a river mentioned in the Puranas, called Shubhsrava. An ancient river: who knows what unknown forests it flows through. What sort of vegetation grows on its banks, what tributaries come and merge with it. Where is its origin: how small, almost imperceptible. Insubstantial in the beginning. Gradually taking on the shape of a river. Full of water, full of plants, full of fish. Full of sound, and brimming with waves of beauty. A river of childhood: a young river in the abode of ancients. A river untouched by gods. A river untouched by geography. A river of only words. A river made up of words. A river that flows beside the pure and radiant, then disappears. A river called Shubhsrava, yet unnamed. A river held in an infant god's scripture. An impossible river, a hidden, a vanished river. A river in Shubhsrava: a river in every river. Flowing from the Puranas down to these words: a river, Shubhsrava.

(1990)

A Carnival of Rivers

There must be a geography in which it's possible for all the world's rivers to come together in a carnival. Most carnivals are held by a river: the carnival of rivers must be held by the sea. For as long as the carnival runs, the sea must rein in its power to consume everything. Rivers small and big must come down arm in arm: the Amazon, the Ganga, the Nile, the Yangtze, and more. Rivers that have never met before. Rivers coming along with their origins and ends. Rivers bringing with them images of all the mountain ranges they flow through. Rivers bringing with them all the wealth of their banks, their flood plains, their vegetation. The Ganga could borrow from the Amazon some forests untouched by the sun, the Amazon could take from the Ganga some shrines and weathered gods.

Before the carnival can end, the rivers must play together as an orchestra: the river Dhasan can sound the first note, the Narmada can join in with the second, a river from Africa could extend the third, and the fourth could echo from the soft sounds of the Loire. The greedy sea must also sneak in its own low rumble. And the god who should have been taking care of the rivers but has been sleeping for centuries, will be woken up by the music of the rivers, not realising that they are coming back from a carnival.

(2012)

Barbarians

They come on chariots, they come on horseback, and sometimes they come unarmed just to look around. They come waving flags saying that we should return to the pure and holy ways of bygone centuries. They come like merchants and lay out their wares. They come with talk of revenge for injustices ages old. They come to demonstrate the importance of preserving your identity. They come chanting prayers, they come singing hymns. And then they kill, they demolish, they destroy. They come to test the limits of your tolerance. They spread out, they tar everything and everyone with the same brush. They frighten. They provoke, they suppress. They come and we welcome them with festoons and garlands, we shower them with flowers. They make us dance like puppets even though they are no puppet-masters. We look on in astonishment as they go about their destruction. They turn us into them and return reassured. They are barbarians – they turn us into barbarians and go back. Then they don't return for a long time. They don't need to.

(1990)

Postscript

Our camp was plundered. Nothing remains. The chieftain who ordered it, it must have been his right. We haven't come to complain about him. We know that camps are plundered every other day – it is the custom here. That our camp was plundered before yours causes us no bitterness. Ours, yours, everyone's camps will be plundered like this, that is their destiny – nothing can be gained from whining and complaining. Whatever remained after the plunder was burned down. Our faces are covered in the dust of being plundered and the ash of being burned. We haven't burned our own house down and come here to look at the spectacle. Actually we haven't come here at all, and no one, not even that chieftain, has sent us. Dust and ash, they blow with the wind – they can't be trained or directed anywhere. Nor are we waiting for you to be plundered and burned. We're just a vagrant, almost vanished camp that has nowhere to go. If we happen to be here, it's only because we happen to be nowhere else. We do not exist, and we're only standing next to that which will not exist. Our camp was plundered.

(1990)

Part IV

In Bhilai

Even there, where a machine chops off
iron's burning outstretched arms with an inhuman
sound
I will sleep soundly
and wake refreshed
without getting tangled up in nightmares –
and unmolested by any sweet word or gesture
I will remember you:
in an endless summer I may forget the seasons
but I will still recognise those fragrant days
when in my arms
your unwearied beauty will flower:
a murderous noise will be all around
and my heart
like molten incandescent iron
will flow towards you on countless paths
that you can keep shaping
to your heart's desires –

Then one night when
your blood and your heart and your love
will start becoming heavy like steel,
I will

call out to you
from under the trains that carry people and coal
from behind the lights that guard sleeping cities:
the earth will be dazed like heavy black fear
the overcast sky will be still like death
and my countless parts will wait for you
near the machine-gates –

(1961)

Possibility

The city is still a possibility
I realised when I touched
Sveta's friendly hands on a busy road
one winter afternoon –
soon my hands forgot that
touch
and returned to me, alone as ever.
In the crowd waiting at the traffic signal
there was no
meaning for my body anywhere,
there was no quiet private warmth anywhere
which I could call my love –
there was only a slight irrelevant breeze
jolted by a stopping bus:
feeling unhappy, I wanted to convey my sympathies
to my hands clutching the handrail
when I remembered the hands
that they'd held just a short while ago,
the body attached to them that had turned
into another body,
and then I found a few words
that I could keep there
where those hands had been –

shivering in a cold gust from the window
my heart
found new hope
for hands
for poetry

the city is still a possibility.

(1963)

The First Kiss

Two leaves of one living stone
blood red, eager
tremble and join,
I see:
I can make flowers bloom

(1960)

Remembering the Sun while Making Love

When the shadows of your lips
approach my lips
and my fingers begin to warm in the sunlight
of your fingers,
then there are only eyes
that await my return
in the days when I did not know
that there's a flower that grows between two hands
– sunflower.

When you stand in a darkened doorway
and toss a song at me
from over your shoulder
and I stand still like a tree,
then there are only eyes
that await my return
in the days when I did not know
that there's a river that flows between two faces
– sunriver.

When you sink into my arms
like the colours of dusk
and I emerge like a reflection in water,
then there are only eyes
that await my return
in the days when I did not know
that there's a sky that exists between two bodies

– sunsky.

(1960)

Come

Come,
as darkness to darkness comes
as water meets water
as light dissolves in light.

Come,
wear me
as the tree wears
its bark
as the trail wears
green grass.

Take me
as darkness takes roots
as water takes the moon
as eternity takes time.

(1984)

Fragrance

Her body fills up with fragrance
like the sky with blue
like the grass with green –

then the world is open like wonder
and like the petals of a flower
time keeps blooming, withering.

(1985)

Only the Body Reveals the Body

Just as the tree
has leaves, bark, trunk, roots
it also has
its own light, its own splendour –
the sun merely reveals it.

The body's light awakens similarly
at love's touch.
The body is a tree
waiting for light –

only the body reveals the body.

(1985)

A Place for Love 1

He made a place for love.

He swept away the stars
pushed aside the sun and moon
cleared the forest vines
dusted and wiped down the earth
and uncreased the sky

he made a place for love.

(1986)

A Place for Love 2

A lonely afternoon
solitude at the edge of a crowded evening
the third seat in a packed bus
– he made a place for love.

He pushed the gods outside
and pled with the birds
to leave him a bit of sky –

he snatched a flower from a child's hand
and borrowed some green from a leaf
amidst butterflies and squirrels and sunlight
he made a place for love.

(1986)

Return

She's here

the air's fragrant with plants and flowers
the rain's soft like small hands
the sun shines on trees unseen
the sky's deserted despite its countless songs

a little girl
forgets her schoolbag
and, chirping, climbs aboard the bus

she's here
the way time comes to eternity
the way good fortune comes to your door
the way dew comes to grass, and sun to dew
the way rain comes to sun, and green to rain

she's here

(1986)

I Touched Her

I touched her
like I touched the sky
like I slipped a star
on her finger as if it were a ring.

Like darkness came to me to say
look, she's the flame of a lamp
like the wind recognised her colour, her glow.

I told good fortune
my arms don't encircle her
she is apart, yet stands with me.

I touched her
like sky like stars
like darkness like light
like I touched good fortune.

(1986)

Stone Makes Love to Stone

In Khajuraho

Stone kisses
stone

stone crushes stone
in its arms

stone fills up stone –

stone caresses
stone

stone is aroused
stone looks on in rapture
stone invites
stone

stone raises its arms
stone pounds stone thighs
stone blossoms into breasts

stone quivers
stone melts
stone gushes out in torrents
stone
sanctifies
stone

stone makes love to stone.

(1987)

How Will She

How will she say yes –
yes
her enraptured eyes
her erect nipples
her body's astonished fragrance
her wet lips
will say yes –
how will she say yes?

(1990)

Nude 1

She was a flame
not still, but vibrant,
quivering.
Not from any timidity
but from a desire she kindled herself.
She with the sparkle of
deep, burning dreams in her eyes.
She with the lustre of her lips.
Like an imprint.
She was low-naveled
– writhing in her own unrestrained excess,
she was a wet flower
hidden behind inky leaves,
waiting in her dark universe
for the bright light of pleasure.

She was a flame
her body a lamp
burning in love
naked.

(1995)

Nude 2

There was nothing to cover her
no sky
no time
no sunlight

but her body's sky was
stretched out like green grass

her body's time was
timeless like the wind

her body's sunlight
shone bright like salt

in her own sky
on her own time
basking in her own sunlight
she
naked.

(1995)

Nude 3

She's a mirror
not her, her nakedness –
and she herself
is reflected in it

Youth sees
its grandeur in that mirror,
beauty gazes
at its boundless splendour,
she's a mirror
not just her, her nakedness...

The sky uncovered
in the dark of night
is its own mirror.

(1995)

Nude 4

In such little space
how can she be the sky
contained but boundless
so close but out of reach
and filled with so many stars?
Dew drenched under her own moon
warmed by her own sun
how can she be the earth
in such little time?

She, naked
not on the bed of earth
nor beneath the sky

she
naked...

(1995)

Nude 5

The earth
takes off
its plants, rivers and valleys

the sky
undoes the knots of stars

the sun
sets aside its fervency

the moon
washes its face in dew

the rock
turns on its side after centuries

time uncovers itself
she is
naked...

(1995)

Nude 6

She couldn't cover her
nakedness
with sweat
with kisses from head to toe
with lovemaking

she covered herself somehow
with her bashfulness
with her own flowering desire.

(1995)

She Said 1

She said
the river's naked,
it doesn't think about shame,
no garment can cover it.

Dark it is
though every morning and evening
it becomes radiant
not from shame, not from pleasure
but from the rising and setting sun.

I am in love,
I'm not a river,
that's why I turn red from shame –
I don't want to flow anywhere
the thing that keeps me here
is love.

(2001)

She Said 2

She said
even under that tree
even in the green dark of leaves
she was the sky –
the red sky of dusk
not blue;
sweat glittered on her body like stars
her eyes, though hesitant, shone.

Someone else was there
spying upon her radiance
who then dissolved into darkness
– it must have been some god or ancient hero
but I didn't tell her that.

(2001)

She Said 3

She said
can the wind wear away a large rock so that
its fragments, its dust can't be found anywhere?

Would that rock remember
that it was under it he touched me years ago
suddenly, and for the first time?

I want to return to that rock,
I want to return his memories and dreams to him.

I know
my heart
is being worn away too
by love and dreams and memories.

(2001)

He Said

He said
I'm coming back soon
that's what he said when he left.

How was I to know
that my path would be covered in rocks and darkness.

I was lost
I couldn't find my way:
the sky may be merciful, but it doesn't give directions.

Bloodied by thorn and scrub
by pit and path
the rock I rested my weariness upon
was my love
– how was I to know?

(2001)

I Say

I say to the trees
Make a palanquin from your green
and bring her to me;

I say to the flowers
Make a palanquin from your pollen
and bring her to me;

I say to the sky
Make a palanquin from your light and shade
and bring her to me;

I say to the birds
Make a palanquin from your wings and chatter
and bring her to me –

I say to the gods I meet at the corner
Carry the palanquin and bring her to me
I am standing at my door to welcome her.

(2003)

Before the Sky

Before the sky
the sun rises in her eyes.
The wonder of the very first sunrise
still lives on under her eyelids.
Her skin is full
of the ecstasy and radiance of the first sunlight:
Looking at her
is like seeing everything happen for the first time.

(2006)

The Other Name for Awakening

In her eyes
is the dense green darkness
that shades the river waters.

The sweat of her palms
is the water of springs flowing silently in forests.

On her lips
is the imprint of dew falling late at night.

At the touch of her hands
colours come alive
shapes come alive
countless heartbeats quicken.

She is the other name for awakening.

(2006)

Time Doesn't Come Here

Time doesn't come here anymore
what comes is death
with its heavy footsteps
through the long, centuries-old corridors
that are wordless and unwaiting.

Sunlight comes
now and then illuminating for no reason
the seams of ancient stones,
dew falls
silently
on the ancient plants and grass
that never wither or dry,
and there the damp stays like a prayer
for a long time past sunrise.

Her footsteps can't be heard
but she comes
before death,
time hidden in the glimmer of her eyes
time wrapped effortlessly around her fingers.
Time doesn't come here
but she does...

(1994)

So Late

Ask her:
why has she come so late?
By now the earth has circled
so many times around the sun,
so many trees have turned to stone,
the dreams of so many stones
have turned to dust and blown away –
epics lie in tatters
and waiting itself has turned grey,
birds have tired of chirping and singing
and have returned to their nests,
words have started moving towards silence,
and the call of death is slowly getting louder –
Ask her
why she has come so late.

(2006)

Part V

The Window Opens but No One Looks Out

The window opens to the outside: it joins the inside to the outside through sight. So that the inside remembers that there is an outside. So that the outside doesn't forget that there is an inside. The window is a simple opportunity for the inside and the outside to acknowledge each other. There is a sky above the house, but sometimes it's visible only through the window. Because of the window, the house remembers the sky. And the sky too becomes an insider by entering the house through the window.

The scene visible outside quietly enters the house through the window. By the same route, a small part of what's happening inside slips outside. Often we are able to see from inside the house, by means of the window, many such things that no one knows we're seeing – neither the one being seen, nor anyone else. The window can be a secret lookout. An eye that sees and that no one else can see. The window knows how to hide secrets and how to let mysteries remain unlocked. The window can be dangerous.

Poetry is a window to the infinitude of the world. An infinitude that we would possibly not have recognised had that window not been there. If we want to, we can look out this window: we can see infinity. But the being of the window, of the scene and of infinity is not dependent on our looking. The window is an invitation to look. It may be that we take too long to accept the invitation. But this delay makes no difference because the infinity that poetry is a window to does not pass.

But looking is also doing – the view that one who sees from afar is not a participant is baseless. In looking, we become involved in the scene. Without us the scene is not complete. In looking at infinity, we become part of it. Poetry is not a boat for crossing the sea of life, it is the foolhardiness of trying to attain infinity from the vortex of this sea. It is the tireless attempt to bring that which is far and beyond, close.

(1994)

By the River Is Also a River

Here, very close, is the river Rhone. On this side is Villeneuve and on that side Avignon. Not now, but last year we sat for a very long time beside it. If you stare at the water flowing past while sitting on the bank, it often feels as if the water is still and the bank is flowing. Sitting by a river is also flowing with the river: often the river is still while we who are sitting on the bank flow. Being near the river is being the river. In one of his poems Vinod Kumar Shukla talks of going to meet the 'river-faced people'. Maybe it is not just those who live by the river who become river-faced, we who sometimes and for a little while only are able to come and sit by the river, we too, if only for a little while, become river-faced. The river ignores no one: it drenches everyone, makes them a part of itself. Even those who go only for a little while become part of the river's clan.

Just like the river, poetry has been with us for centuries. Waters come from everywhere and merge with it: it keeps emptying into the sea every day but never runs out of water. In poetry too, all sorts of images, word-play, descriptions and beliefs come from everywhere and merge. The way the river never empties of water, poetry never empties of words. Near the river and near poetry we cannot remain indifferent: if we approach them in earnest then we cannot escape being overwhelmed. We are included in the river and in poetry despite ourselves. The way the river's splendour lights up our faces, in the same way our faces shine with poetry. Continuity, both in the river and in poetry, showers our mortality with eternity.

A line from a poem goes: 'What sort of river are you?' One answer could be: "The sort of poem you are!'

(1994)

Mud-Soaked Shoes

Years ago I read a poem by Tadeusz Różewicz in which there was talk of entering heaven with mud-soaked shoes. Then too, it was not the contrast, but the image of the shoes that attracted me more. From it emerged the picture of a working man, a hard worker toiling all day.

There has been much debate about the relation poetry has to our daily working lives. From the insistence that poetry should accurately and with feeling depict this life, to the notion that poetry exists in its own world of fevered imagination and has nothing to do with the real world. But it is true that if there are images in poetry from the life we recognise, it is easier to relate to. These images, though, should not be mere imitation. If poetry does not minutely, imaginatively and in unexpected ways expand and rediscover them, then poetry will never become richer. The ordinary reader goes to poetry to sharpen and deepen his own awareness of what life feels like. And also to know what life can feel like. True poetry does not take us away from life: it makes our involvement in it deeper and more complex. But it gives us respite from the daily drudgery and anxiety. Instead of getting trapped in the everyday, we are able to go to a place not far from it which we were otherwise not able to see or know.

Poetry does not scorn the everyday: it does not ignore the drudgery of the day-to-day either. It excites or illuminates the routine of life in such a way that what is not everyday or routine also becomes part of it. If poetry is able to reach some mature understanding or vision or philosophy, it is only with the help of the everyday – by going through the unavoidable drudgery of the day-to-day. Poetry enters heaven with mud-soaked shoes.

(1994)

The Grass Calling Out to the Galaxy

Chamber 'M' of the chartreuse I am in was made in the fourteenth century and for hundreds of years Christian monks had lived in it. Then the French Revolution came and they were pushed out. Behind every chamber is a porch on which green grass grows. Opposite is a tall ancient monument where pigeons congregate. High above it is the sky.

The grass must have always been here. It must have yellowed, dried and then grown again. The grass here in this monastery is the same as time. Passing very slowly yet always there – just like the grass.

The grass is very low: often there is nothing else, only grass. As if nothing or no one is present nearby, only words: not words spoken by someone, but those gathered inside oneself, raging or timid.

Sunlight falls on the grass, darkness gathers, dew falls. The wind goes by, caressing it. When no one knows, the grass looks to the sky. It may be close to the ground, nevertheless it talks to the galaxy which is nothing else but grass growing in the porch of the sky.

The grass tells the galaxy what is in its green heart and the galaxy tells the grass of its glowing experiences. Poetry sometimes hears this conversation and remembers it. And through it we are sometimes able to hear fragments of this secret conversation.

Poetry gives us the location of many such conversations. If it weren't for poetry we would not even have imagined that the grass was calling out to the galaxy.

(1994)

No Name for the Green Leaf

In the chartreuse there are many porches and courtyards. There, besides the green grass, are trees and plants. A few rose vines have tags saying that they are ancient roses. Who knows how many centuries old they are, but still eager to be green and to flower. In a centuries-old flowerbed there blossoms today's rose, its green vine.

Adjacent to that vine is a tree. That too has a tag with a name. But the name is the tree's. Its beautiful green-pink leaf lay fallen on the ground and I picked it up. All its veins show clearly. But it has no name of its own. It is not just another leaf: it has an unparalleled beauty – its aura is different. But it has no name: it's just a leaf of a certain tree. All of our features are similar but we all have different names. Man is more unjust to things than to other men. He does not give them the many different names they deserve.

Poetry resists this continual injustice, wants to redress the wrong done to things. It tries to give a name to every leaf. Poetry is the unconditional acceptance of the individuality of being. For it, everything is alive: the beloved, the window, the ladybird wandering in the grass, the forgotten leaf-covered statue of a god, the fallen leaf in a dense forest. It is the tireless, unceasing process of giving everything a name. Poetry does not group things into classes or divisions. It searches for a name for every form. If poetry did not make this attempt we would not have known so much that is unique. Poetry is not just the artistic conservation of individuality but also its moral conservation.

(1994)

The Sunlight Asked Me

It has been raining since morning today. A light rain and everything is foggy. It seems as if it is still night. Not a completely dark night, but a long dawn – there is light but it does not encroach upon the darkness. The sun comes a bit late anyway. Only after nine in the morning does it shine upon the grapes. Mist is settling upon the window panes. Nowhere is there a hint or suspicion of sunlight. Still, there is the wait for it. Without sunlight it is difficult to believe that the day has arrived. Our conversation with the day takes place through sunlight. If there is no sunlight, it is as if the day becomes dumb, almost speechless.

Here, in this old Christian monastery, it is peaceful. Ancient piety, with its secrets, fear and silence. When sunlight comes it feels as if some connection has been made with the outside world. This monastery too is liberated from its old seclusion by the sunlight. When there is no sunlight, then not even the sound or chirping of birds can be heard. A cold wind blows, but it's outside. When there is no sunlight, then even the colours of things dissolve into the sweeping greyness. Sunlight is an opportunity for things to reveal themselves in their many colours.

Because of sunlight we know time. But sunlight goes right through time. It covers our past, our present, our future, as if all at once. For it everything is at once, not one after another. All our time gathers in the sunlight. Today there is no sunlight and so this monastery is in the fog of the fourteenth century and we are on the slope of the twentieth. Tomorrow, when there is sunlight, it will shine on all these centuries, on the space between them and on us, all at once. Sunlight has no history: it liberates us from history too. Shapes, ideas, constructs, customs, forms, desires, all keep changing but sunlight does not. The sunlight now is the same as it always was and the same as it always will be.

The sunlight doesn't talk to me directly. It talks through the grass, the shapes of buildings, the flowers, people, children, women, birds, shadows, etc. and I feel as if the sunlight has asked me something or said something to me.

(1994)

A God in Your Luggage

A poem by the French poet Alain Bosquet ends with these lines:

If you have come here to stay
then don't forget to bring
a god in your luggage

Reading this poem here, in the dwelling place of some fourteenth century monk in this chartreuse in Villeneuve, is almost a sin. Although poetry is above sin and virtue. There are very few poets who claim to be virtuous. Even the saint-poets often say things like 'no one is as devious, wicked and lustful as me'. It's said Milton wanted to justify the ways of god to man in his epic, but instead, *Paradise Lost* justifies the ways of the devil. Sin is more attractive to poetry than virtue. In sin there are perhaps more possibilities of exploring and discovering the world in its entirety, in all the colours of its being.

Poetry thinks of everything as a creation: nature creates a lot of things, the rest, man creates. God, deities, etc. are also his creations. Poetry puts the whole stuff of man on the scales: it keeps track of what he takes on his travels. It knows that gods are not self-begotten. They are needed, but they have to be created. They are not there already: wherever we settle, that place needs some sanctity, some invulnerability. That is why poetry tells us to not forget to bring a god along with the rest of our belongings. The way we need grain and water, taste and smell, joy, etc. to live, in the same way we need sanctity. But it will not come by itself, nor will anyone insist on giving it to us. We will have to bring it with us. In the end, we create our god ourselves. He is our own secret. Poetry reminds us to bring and keep with ourselves our sanctity and our secret.

(1994)

Knocking, but No One at the Door

Here, in this Christian monastery turned into a monument, there is incredible peace. Hours go by, but no one passes through its long deserted corridors. In the day, some tourists' voices can be heard: sometimes the laughter or screams of children. If someone comes, their footsteps can be heard a long time beforehand and for a long time after. It is so deserted that, in the words of Ghalib, 'if you die there will be no one to mourn or cry'. This really is 'such a place' where 'there is no one'. Maybe there is god, a holy fear, maybe the hovering spirits of Christian monks, though not one of them gives proof of his presence. The chamber's door remains closed and no one comes up to it. Still, now and then, it feels as if someone has knocked. Very lightly, the way children sometimes mischievously do and disappear. We can never be completely alone: maybe because we are afraid to. We want to get rid of our loneliness, our solitude, our isolation: we want someone to call us, talk to us. We want someone to remember that we exist despite being enclosed in this solitude. We do not want to remain locked in this edifice of our isolation, that is why, now and then, we hear a knock which is not there, when there is no one. We ourselves are knocking on the door of our solitude. That is why we hear knocking, but no one is at the door. Sometimes we want to come out of ourselves just to meet ourselves.

Is poetry just such a knock on the dense solitude of the soul? It inspires us to open the door and go meet ourselves. It is not a knock of time, or a call to attention, or one that tells us to get ready to go somewhere. It does not alert us to danger. It is a knock of being: it is a knock that reminds the inside of the outside. It is a knock that connects permanence to presence. When we ignore the knocking of poetry, or when we can't even hear it, then either an unbreakable harmony has formed within and without us, as in a deity or a saint, or we have stopped living in our solitude.

(1994)

Part VI

God

I hadn't seen him
but I felt him walk beside me
on that street familiar even in the dark.
– When I hid from the lights
of approaching cars
        from fear of being recognised
then I could hear somewhere near
        the sound of music –
and later when I entered the building
and stumbled on the staircase
from nervousness and excitement
then I felt as if he had steadied me.
In the perfumed darkness of the room
she was delirious with anticipation
and as we kissed
we felt grateful
that he was somewhere outside
        standing guard.
Slowly as we forgot him
and became consumed by each other
when we frantically began to search
for the face of our child still lost in the future
there was a sound like a knock on the door
and I felt

that someone had woken up
and he was warning us –
when I softly stepped outside
after quickly giving her one last kiss
in the twilight
I saw him – I saw him for the first time:
his dark slender body was panting
his face sunken, his eyes lowered
he seemed to be holding castanets
he was standing
behind a crowd that carried sticks and knives and flags
and behind him
somewhere far away
        the hymns of dawn.

(1962)

I Want

A small house won't do,
I want the whole earth
surrounded by
its plants and seas and people.

A window won't suffice,
I want the whole sky
filled with its countless stars and planets.

This little lamp can't quell
my darkness
I want
a brilliant, blazing sun.

A few words are not enough
to make a poem,
I want all of language –
all the green of the earth
all the blue of the sky
all the red of sunrise.

(1987)

After the End 1

After the end
we won't sit quiet.

We'll quarrel again,
we'll seek again,
leap over boundaries again.

Earth water fire
wind and sky
we'll tell them again –
come,
give us form,
give us shape.

The same as before
the same
that the end thinks
it has erased forever.

After the end
we won't be finished –
we'll hover here
close to life –
blossoming like scent,

flowing like air,
gathering like memory.

In the end
we'll evade the end
and come here again –
after the end
we won't sit quiet.

(1990)

After the End 2

After the end
there'll be nothing –
no coming back
no transformation
no new beginning.

After the end
there'll only be the end.

No startled moonrise of the body,
no dark night of the soul,
no sunlit memory of love.

No weak, watered-down tea,
nor the annoyance
of buttonholes smaller than buttons.

No tree of words,
no lake of silence,
no old iniquities,
no blue feathers falling silently in the forest.

No gods without halos,
no flag-waving goons.
After the end
there'll be nothing for us –
they who have no end
will have everything.

After the end
there'll only be
the end,
for us.

(1990)

Hope Chooses 'Perhaps'

Hope chooses a small word for itself
'perhaps' –

When it sounds like a man in uniform
is knocking at the door in the middle of the night
to investigate a crime that has not been committed
hope crouches in a dark corner
like a pet cat
thinking it's only the wind
perhaps.

Amidst the earsplitting hymns
to a suspect god buried in flowers
and the greasy smell of oil and ghee
hope flickers
like some forgotten mantra
perhaps under the half-cooked offerings and sticky devotion
some ancient holiness still survives.

When it seems as if the merciless truck
coming down the crowded street at reckless speed
will run over
the little girl who has appeared out of nowhere

then hope
like a decrepit old woman
will pounce upon her
and carry her to safety
scattering the festooned stalls
of destiny and accident.

Perhaps is a word
that fell suddenly like a flower
from the bakauli tree that shaded so many childhood games
perhaps is a stone that someone threw in anger
at not scoring well in the exams –
perhaps is a window from which
the slowly fading image of a beloved was seen
perhaps is the unburnt bone
that we forgot
at the pyre
after cremating a friend
and which still hasn't found a river.

Hope has chosen
a small, weary word
'perhaps'.

(1991)

Near

Near the stone was the tree
near the tree was the bush
near the bush was the grass
near the grass was the earth
near the earth was the high cliff
near the cliff was the fort's tower
near the tower was the sky
near the sky was the void
near the void was the cosmic sound
near the sound was the word
near the word was the stone
each was near the other
but time was near none

(1994)

Far

Far from the window was the temple wall
far from the wall was the narrow lane
far from the lane was the water source
far from the source was the forest
far from the forest was the settlement
far from the settlement was the graveyard
far from the graveyard was the garden
far from the garden was the school
far from the school were sins
far from sins was poetry
far from poetry was prayer
far from prayer was god
far from god were words
far from words was absence
they all were far
yet close to time –

(1994)

I Want Words

There's green grass growing on the graves of six hundred
Christian monks
from the still living house of one among them
from the still intact wilderness without words that they
created
not far from his own death but alive for now
the six hundred and first, a poet
waiting, not to be buried in the namelessness of the earth
but to be burned bone by bone under the open sky
am searching for
words for my poetry
everlasting holiness for words
a bustling happy home for holiness
and a way to help me survive for a few more days
the lacklustre rocks have no answer
the windows that open onto solitude
can't see beyond the overcast sky and deserted street
an amnesiac sadness sits upon the soggy rain-drenched
bodies of chairs
neither gods, nor god's messengers, nor holy words can
be seen in the light
what's visible are corridors abandoned by monks,
windows cut to the beat of prayer,
earthworms wriggling in the grass, carefree tourists,

lovers pawing at each other in a corner
and sometimes a cat staring like death from the bastion
I want words
the hope that they might live on after me
at least for a while
I don't want a waning sunlight, but one that flowers
not prayers but a call
not silence but a scream
sobs, tears, laughter
I don't want glory, I want words

(1994)

Fisherman

Now, if it was discovered that
the sky is really a vast net

cast into the invisible waters
of the universe to catch
the sun, the moon, the stars and constellations, the earth
and planets
by someone who then fell asleep
would you still call him a fisherman?
It's quite likely that he had another, nicer name
but neither he nor anyone else remembers it
nor do we, although it's also quite likely that he is our
ancestor.

Casting a net is like making a guess
how can we know
what truth we'll catch this time?
When the net grows heavy
when we pull it out and see it filled
with the squirming silver of fish
then our eyes, too, shine like the fish
because coming so far out to sea in this little boat
unarmed
was not in vain.

It's hard to tell,
at least it's hard for us,
whether what's in the net,
what's suffering and squirming and will soon be still,
is time or truth or just some fish.

We come early, before the crack of dawn even
in our boats out to sea.
Sometimes the sun jumps out of the east
like a giant fish
luminous, tinged with red, slipping away from our
hands.

This life, submerged in water but pulsing and boundless –
this water, calling out with it's numberless voices –
these countless, ever-changing colours of water, of sky,
of fish –
these underwater plants, softly singing –
to flow, to flow along and never find a shore –
this constant struggle against water
arms and oars and boats tearing through it –
and me
with my net:
why does it feel as if all of this never passes
that it doesn't have any history?
It just is: and it will remain.

Sometimes when I'm sitting in my boat feeling low,
I think:
just as we don't live in order to die
in the same way fish aren't born for us to eat –
why does someone or the other, sooner or later, have to
devour all beautiful things?
Why are the truths, of water, net, boat and fish, opposed
to each other?
It's not that the times have changed:
it was always so.
Just like this truth: that in the end
we are all caught in each others' nets
and at any moment the only question is
who will eat whom first.

I know how to catch fish
but if I ever get caught in some net
then just like my helpless fish
I would not know how to escape.

I don't know much about centuries
although on occasion I read
tales of war etc. with interest.
But this terrifying century
it feels as if
man has caught a crocodile in his net instead of fish
and it's now trying to devour him.

There's no way out except to kill it
and cast the net again
so that the next century can come like a beautiful fish
which we can then return lovingly to the sea.

The very first fisherman had love in his heart
and the very last fisherman too
will try to save what's beautiful
– for that's what being human is all about.

(1998)

The Passing of Things

I want to watch the passing of things
how every moment passes,
how every letter scatters,
how every petal withers.

I want to try and save
beauty from time,
my path from merging with any other road,
my truth from perishing within me,
my voice from trembling with fear.

I want to try
and save
a chapter of the *Hitopadesha* from my childhood
textbook,
a love song remembered in darkness but not sung,
the impossible sweetness of the lives of poor children
pouncing on leftovers at the sweetmeat seller's,
the words of a prayer recalled after the time for prayer
has passed.

In the blazing eyes of refugees whom hardship has aged
before their time
I want to try and draw a map of home and homeland:

as I teach my grandson the alphabet
I want to repeat again –
the letters of hope still shining
on the torture bed of my slowly dwindling time.

I want to watch the passing of things
how every moment passes,
how every letter scatters,
how every petal withers.

(2001)

Prayer 1

I have loved, not prayed
I've chosen holy words, written poetry, not prayed;
grateful, I have touched the earth;
distressed, I have called out to the sky;
I've held water in my hands many times;
surrendered myself to the wind;
let my life warm in the heat of fire;
I have not prayed.
I've stood by people;
left grain for birds;
envied the fortune of others but not their fame;
I've stayed alone and practiced silence;
been always prepared to leave;
never given up the will to live;
led many to the temple;
saw belief cause destruction;
witnessed generosity, not vengeance, after torture;
I've never calculated –
I couldn't understand the mathematics of life.

In the dark verandas of dreams
in the paternal bower of memory
in the deserted arena of desire
I have seen them wandering now and then, they who
could have been gods:
I have not prayed.

(2001)

Prayer 2

If you can
just once
grant me a life that's not my own.
That I may always have shelter for a night
in someone else's home,
a bed, a table, a plate of food, a glass of water.
Let no one wait for me
but when I get there may I find
that I am not unwelcome.
Let only my most basic needs be fulfilled
but allow me the extravagance
of waking up at dawn to store away a bit of sunshine.

If I get lost in the cold, dark forest
let me find some cave where
the embers from a fire
still smoulder in a corner
and where dreams don't turn into ghosts
but circle me and stand guard.
Let no one recognise me in the street
but give me the strength to help the elderly

carry their burden home
though it soil my back.

If you can
just once grant me a life where I do not need
to bow my head or kneel for anything,
a life that is itself a wordless prayer.

(2001)

Prayer 3

My prayer comes back
with me
like my sorrow.

I can't leave it with the sunlight
nor with the old beggar
nor with the laughing child who lives nearby;
my prayer comes back.

There's no time for my prayer;
it asks for no deliverance.

There's no place for my prayer;
it cannot stay in the temple,
it has no place in the geography of words.

Sorrow is joined so closely to my prayer
that it has become my prayer's structure.

When god comes to take account
there'll be no record of my prayer in his books,
like my sorrow it will have
already come back to me.

(2001)

Prayer 4

Grant me just this much
that I may, without embarrassment
lift my head up
instead of bowing it in prayer.

(2001)

What Remains, What's Passed

Auschwitz 1

I want to be able to see what remains
the way I see what's passed
like a yellow breach in a field of green.

No, I wasn't there that midnight
when they filled them into carts like cattle
and took them to slaughter with such efficiency,
such care
as if taking innocents to a temple
for some essential morning ritual.

It's true, I didn't stand there smoking oblivious
when that child was thrown into a ditch
like a useless old utensil
fit for the trash heap.
I never picked up words
like charred bones from a mound of ashes
nor did I hide them like suppurating wounds:
I didn't listen to music by soft light
filtering through a lampshade made of human skin –
still
why do I feel responsible;

why do I feel that if I had been there that midnight
I would have watched fearfully
as my neighbours were carted away;
that I would have made a craven prayer
to god, whom I don't believe in
and I would have washed my language clean
of mud and blood and fear;
that I would have cowered at home and written
a safe poem about a sunny day.

I wasn't there but if I were
I would have stayed silent.
That is why I want to see what remains the way I see
what's passed
like a yellow breach in a field of green.
I want to hear the silent scream in my prayer.

(2001)

If Possible

Auschwitz 2

If possible
I want to create a new alphabet of hope
for my time:
where do I begin? 'A' –
from a newborn baby's cry in a three-foot-high shed,
or a bird waiting for its mother in the cavity of some tree
in the snowy wilderness?

'T' – from that young man presenting himself to die
before anyone else at the concentration camp,
or the lines that those awaiting death
dug with their nails into the prison walls?

'N' I write –
from the cane and glasses and charkha
that remained resolute in the face of terror,
or the girl who lost everything but still was helping
a bloodied old woman find her home?

Now when the crown of injustice is glittering
when the statues of the cruelest faces have been moved

from crossroads to museums
when hate spreads out across the earth like a carefully
planned garden
when we're not in jail but still are prisoners of our own
pettinesses –
in reply to my grandson's lisped, 'What are you doing?'
I want to create a new alphabet of hope
on the sullied black slate of history
in which all the world's children
can write their words without hesitation or fear.

(2001)

What They Had

Auschwitz 3

They didn't have salt,
words had deserted them,
they had no memory of relief or aid.

They weren't at home but in a paddock,
they had nothing to do
except wait,
they were gaunt, starving, thirsting
but they had to become gaunter still, and vanish into
smoke.

Their heads were bent in despair,
their arms yellow and powerless,
their lips dry and withered,
they didn't have the time or energy for prayer:
prayer was no longer their home
or their camp.

They didn't have a decked-up god
to parade during worship:
they'd left him outside
like old, worn-out shoes –
naked, carrying a bar of soap,
heading towards death:
all they had was a darkling 'No'.

(2001)

Horses

From beyond the horizon
where stars and comets glitter
like tall grass
the horses come
with trampling hooves
and sculpted muscles
riderless
but as though they are
returning to their camp:
like weary warriors
we see them coming
as if their arrival is an omen
of the end of war.

From beyond the mountains
from unknown valleys
the horses come
as if they're coming home
as if we're waiting to
load them up and start moving
towards our next destination.

The horses come
from all ten directions
carrying some sky on their backs
carrying some stars
wanting good for the earth
astonishing with their speed
the horses come –
unexpected words come to poetry;
light sudden between clouds;
god in crowds.
The horses come.

(2001)

Words Watch Over Us

Words watch over us:
they fall weightless
upon the soul.

In the darkness
by some invisible light
they manage to find
steps amidst thorn and scrub,
a passage through the wilderness,
a window from which to escape
imprisonment by murderers.
They weave a rope
that can be used
to climb out of a blind pit
or to rescue someone
who has fallen into a well.

Sometimes when we're on the wrong path
words prod us
like a nail in the shoe:
they may not be able to stop us
but they let us know
that there are other paths we can take.

Words, heavy like stones
grind themselves into dust
and spread themselves out
so that when we do fall
we don't hurt ourselves.

Words watch over us.

(2003)

No More Words

I have no more words:
just a few helping verbs, a couple of indeclinables
and some silences and sobs.
I saw from a distance
words
lying in pools of blood –
burnt by fire, turned to ashes,
groaning, wounded,
hoping for respite,
amidst the debris
of demolished shops and fallen houses.
Some with innocent childlike faces
were lying in the dump like trash –
I couldn't find the courage to pick them up
and write a poem about these barbaric times.

I wasn't naive,
I kept myself informed, alert –
I knew that people became bloodthirsty at the
slightest excuse
I would hear massacres being planned in the
marketplace, in homes:
I kept quiet
because I believed
that language would remain sacred still.

A rotting, burning stench emanates from language –
it's covered in blood and rags and brutally broken bones:
prayer has turned into a terrible curse
neighbourhoods are places of murder, streets are
galleries of violence
those who were our own until yesterday have been
othered today:
there are no bloodstains on the murderers' faces but the
aura of victory
I watch helpless at how words are sullied,
how hate is woven into the structure of language,
how the neighbourhood is cast out of poetry.

(2003)

Where Should I Pick My Words From?

Where should I pick my words from:
from the games that innocent children play
on the deserted streets of a city in curfew,
from the eyes blazing with hatred
of a woman who has lost everything,
from the bleeding wounds of citizens
who have been wounded for no reason,
where should I pick my words from?

From the heated kisses of lovers lying on the green grass
by a river,
from the ecstatic laughter of leaves and flowers,
from the despairing prayers
that have echoed in god's house for centuries,
where should I pick my words from?

From the last screams of women and children who died
before their time,
from the lying reports of spies,

from the universe whimpering in its impenetrable void,
from the silence of helpless rocks drowning in the river,
from countless unwritten poems,
from wells that have survived in ancient cities,
from the fate of a star that's vanished from the sky,
where should I pick my words from?

(2012)

To Know the Unknowable

I had words
but they couldn't help me know
my bloodthirsty times
my mortal fate
my failed spirit.

I had words
but they couldn't help me know
the boundless unknowable
spread out from here to there.

I had words
but they couldn't help me make
a small hut
to live in.

I had words
but they couldn't open
the path that goes
from being
to nonbeing.

I had words –

(2012)

How

How can I stop here...
beside this river,
on the shore of the sky's infinite blue
near this fistful of words?

How can I say
that this is enough
what I have seen and endured is enough
and now I can take my leave?

How can I believe
that I have said and done
all that I could
and nothing remains?

The world is limitless and beautiful still –
Many silences need to speak out still –
Many people are honest and helpful still –
I haven't revelled in my childhood still.
And morning's blue bird
hasn't picked a twig for her nest
still.

(2012)

A Little Sorrow

May I take a little sorrow with me
to fold carefully into a poem –
I forgot to ask my deceased father
out of fear and hurry.
The dining table was in the veranda
a flowerless harsingar tree in the garden
and Didiya in the kitchen –
I forgot to ask them all
if I could take a little sorrow with me
like peanuts in my pocket.

I brought it away
and no one even noticed:
now it lies with me, old and stale,
it couldn't find a place even in poetry.

(2014)

Verge

I want to tell him that
it isn't right to stay silent at this time,
but I say:
it's been a long time since you came this way.
I want to tell him that
we can't be sitting doing nothing at this point,
but I say:
it's good to go walking in the morning.
I want to tell him that
we have to make it difficult for them,
but I say:
the roads are in terrible shape these days.
I can't tell him and he doesn't understand:
we stand on the verge of our words.

(2014)

My Language Is Shrinking

It's been a long time since I talked to the sunrise
the sun comes quietly and
goes away without a word
the leaves tremble in the wind
and if they speak they can't be heard
the pigeons whisper indistinctly
evening comes and goes
and hums no song –
my language is shrinking.

(2015)

Is, Isn't

This house is and also isn't
the way the earth is
and also isn't –
I picked the rising sun and
hid it in the cave of clouds:
that sunrise was and also wasn't.

I wove a song from the voices of flowers
from the trembling of leaves
from the dark silence of roots –
that song is and also isn't.

What is also isn't:
the magic of being surrounds
the mystery of nonbeing.
That magic is and also isn't,
that mystery is and also isn't –

There are words and syntax
images and the silences between them –
this poem is
and also isn't.

Who can say when
we will escape this maze
of being and nonbeing –
will we, won't we, won't we not?

(2015)

The End

A bed a mattress a pillow
a little light a window
a door to come and go in and out by
some water a glass a cellphone
a couple of books a little silence now and then
lots of voices
a bit of music
a painting on the wall in front of me that I can't
see clearly
some pills scattered on a table
many half-poems in my head
a few words that have returned after ages:
– is this the song the end will sing?

(2015)

P.S.

Insights,
Interviews
&
More ...

Q&A

By Dhruv Shukla

Poetry seems to be a disappearing genre of expression in our times. How do you feel having practised it for nearly six decades?

Poetry may seem to be disappearing but, in fact, it never does. It has become over time a minority activity. It somehow survives all crises and vicissitudes. The green grass asserts itself, every now and then, even though it lies crushed under a tarred road with no chance of survival! One does feel disappointed. But in our times poetry itself is some kind of hope. Perhaps, to borrow the title of the new book by Terry Eagleton, 'hope without optimism'. As for myself, I have survived largely because of poetry: not merely mine but quite substantially of others'.

The number of people who still read and enjoy poetry is small. What you think sustains their abiding interest?

The number is indeed small in many languages including Hindi but it is quite large in Urdu, Malayalam, Bengali, not to speak of languages in Latin America and Africa. Those who are vulnerable to poetry find in poetry their own voice, some kind of moral toughness, certain emotional complexity, intellectual vigour, spiritual solace and, above all, delight in discovering in language new ranges of experience and articulation. A kind of wisdom or insight.

Poetry writes or speaks to its times. Don't you think our times are too complex, confusing and fast-moving for poetry to capture them?

Poetry does speak to and write its time. But it also speaks to the timeless, to eternity. Perhaps it writes less of history, more of eternity. Pasternak said that 'poets are envoys of eternity held hostage by time!' All times, come to think of them, are, have been complex and confusing. Our times are equally so but also very fast-moving. Poetry has tried to cope with all these by inventing new poetic strategies and rhythms, new imagery and structures of complexity. Poetry in some sense always fails its times, but then, times also keep failing poetry. Our times and our poetry are no exceptions.

You started writing poetry in a small central Indian town and now you've been living in a metropolis for more than two decades. Has location influenced your poetry? If yes, in what ways?

Locations matter a lot. A lot of poetry collected in my first volume was about being a young poet in a small town. Local details, the smell of dust, earth, trees, houses and people all mattered. Images come from locations; even memory is deeply rooted in them. I have lived for a short while in Paris, Krakow, Avignon and Nantes. In Avignon I wrote a whole book of poems and prose pieces in about three weeks! Also, nearly a new book of poems in Nantes, where I was for about two months. A lot of poems were written while I was in Paris and Krakow. I would like these poems to be read as tributes to these various locations as well.

Besides poetry, over the years, you have been writing criticism of poetry and literature, of the visual arts and Hindustani classical music. Do they have some organic relationship or do the two exist in mutual discomfort or tension?

In criticism you are basically trying to understand, analyse, possibly judge what others are doing. I have found that criticism is part of my creativity, it is its extension. I hope that in my criticism, largely of poetry, I am able to seize the other for the readers, giving them a taste of what is happening in a work, a book or a trend. Since I remain basically a poet, I try to minimize the area of judgement (the Bible aptly said: 'Judge not for ye shall be judged!') and try to maximise the area of description. But you invariably describe only that which you have judged to be significant and meaningful. My criticism of the visual arts and Hindustani classical music has been structured around poetic celebrations. For long I have felt that our classical music has not received the kind of critical attention, analysis and theorisation which its depth and richness, its dynamism and quiet changes, demand and deserve. I particularly value my book on the vocalist, Kumar Gandharva, and the tome on the iconic Indian painter, Syed Haider Raza. Incidentally, I have written a large number of poems on artists, both visual and musical. I have a whole book of poetry devoted to them. In short, the arts have brought 'the other life' to me and I've been overwhelmed by them and attempted to convey these overwhelming experiences and insights both creatively and critically.

In poetry you are a loner: away from the current idioms you've chosen an idiom, neoclassical in some way, with resonances of culture. Has this isolation from the social to the personal and spiritual been difficult to practise and sustain?

I do not know if I am a loner but I strongly believe that poetry is a way of accessing and exploring the vastly complex relationship between the self and the world. A large part of this world consists of memory, cultural and racial. Also, in the current situation, the personal is being constantly denied its autonomy, facing suppression in the name of the so-called social reality. Faced with this situation, I decided that as a poet my arena would be the personal, the spiritual which resonate with memory. In the voice of a poet his/her ancestors must also speak. I tried doing that and was dubbed elitist, immune to present-day realities and almost anti-social. I write out of deep love and lure for life, others, nature, people, relationships etc. In the existing ethos of the ideological and the obvious, if you do not subscribe to it, you are bound to be an outcast. I have been one. A certain elegance, if you please, is unacceptable and also bound to be misunderstood and misrepresented. Complexity and subtlety as well. I am a neoclassist, if at all, in this sense.

Hindi poetry in the last three-four decades has been dominated by Marxist ideology, its insistence on social reality, and you've been accused of being anti-Marxist and anti-social. How have you coped with these critical accusations?

Accusations apart, I believe ideologies of all kinds inevitably tend to colonise areas of creativity and imagination. They invariably do not allow 'truths' to be discovered through experience and expression but force predetermined structures and rob poetry and literature the thrill of discovery and imagination. Only those writers, those literary works, matter which are able to go beyond their ideological constraints, exceed or supercede them. There have been some major figures in Hindi whose work did exactly this and cannot be explained or defended in terms of ideology, namely Muktibodh, Shamsher Bahadur Singh, Raghuvir Sahay, Shrikant Verma and Krishna Sobti.

That said, I am aware that even Marxism has produced great literature when it was not in power or less tyrannical, such as in Latin America and East European countries. Pablo Neruda, Vasko Popa, Zbignew Herbert, Miroslav Holub, Nazim Hikmet, Bertolt Brecht etc. are names to reckon with.

There are many ways of looking at, understanding and changing the world. No ideology can claim to have a monopoly of social change and social reality. Agyeya, Nirmal Verma (Hindi), U.R. Ananthamurthy (Kannada), Arun Kolatkar (Marathi), Shankho Ghosh (Bengali), Rama Kant Rath (Oriya) etc. are major Indian figures who did not owe allegiance to any rigid ideology.

Though I was attacked as an anti-Marxist, I never failed to acknowledge the best of Marxists. In fact, for the last thirty years or so, I've been proposing a great trinity of Hindi poetry of the last half century consisting of Agyeya, Shamsher and Muktibodh, the last two owing express allegiance to Marxism. In my journals and other fora of dialogue and discussion, I always invited Marxists and they thankfully participated. My quarrel was with the many Marxist writers organisations which created a climate of intolerance, parochialism and ideological untouchability. Under their influence, many young writers exiled personal reality, love etc. from their writings. I opposed it and continue to do so even now.

Your insistence on the autonomy of poetry, on the freedom of the republic of imagination, has received wide attention and scathing attacks. Why this assertion of autonomy?

When literature is being reduced to being seen as a colony of ideas generated elsewhere and basically as an ideological construct, I found it imperative to insist that while ideas do play a role and find a place in literature, it is not primarily read and appreciated for its ideas. Second, literature in itself is a genre of reflection on life, self, the human condition and the world. Third, literature is politics enough, spirituality enough. And while it is always in dialogue with politics, religion, ideology etc., it resists their dominance.

Does the notion of autonomy of literature relieve it of any social responsibility or awareness? Would you describe yourself as a socially aware poet?

No, it does not, it only redefines it. Autonomy does not mean any kind of autocracy or tyranny. It means freedom, which is always surrounded by all kinds of restrictive realities, including social and personal. Freedom would have a place and meaning if society in general has an ethos which permits and promotes, and, if need be, protects it. Literature is written by individuals out of their own choice, but it needs others, a society which would listen and respond to its voice. Let me also remind you that in tyrannical societies and times, literature has often provided a way out, an avenue to freedom. My insistence on the personal in a climate in which the social is being allowed to trample or subdue the personal, its rehabilitation, is a radically social act. The personal cannot survive without the social, the social acquires meaning by being personal as well. In some sense, the dichotomy is baseless.

Another concept you've insisted upon is that of language. You've a large number of poems about language and word. Is there a historical or cultural context to this emphasis on language or is it merely a personal choice?

The classical Indian view has been that the universe was created out of five elements – earth, water, fire, ether and wind. I add language as the sixth element, which makes earth a world for us. Language, together with god, time and abstraction are four radical inventions of Homo sapiens. All other inventions i.e. science, knowledge etc. are footnotes to the central invention of language. Language is under jeopardy in our times the world over. It is being flattened, simplified, reduced to shallowness, intellectual and emotional vacuity by political discourse, media etc. Literature is one area where language in all its complexity, humanness, grandeur and possibility could be saved, animated and preserved. This is the broader context in which I emphasise the importance of language. A reduction of its importance and power would be a devaluation of our humanity. We are different from animals only because we have language. The insistence is, no doubt, also a personal choice.

You have lived through a long and exciting phase of modernism and now perhaps in a period of post-modernism. How has the passage been?

No passage is ultimately smooth. Each one is beset with difficulties and problems. The modern is a permanent presence. In India, for instance, the Indian term for the modern was used for the first time in the tenth century by a new school of Nyaya philosophy. Similarly, even in the post-modern, the modern persists. The modern made it more open, inclusive, democratic, by admitting vastly differing viewpoints. But it also brought a certain chaos, a kind of anarchy. While one may welcome the opening up, the liberalization, succumbing to chaos and anarchy is difficult and continues to constitute a major problem.

You have been deeply interested, and unusually involved, in the arts. Has this influenced your poetry?

The arts for me have been a way of coming in touch with 'the other life', 'the other reality'. Very enriching, emotionally exciting, intellectually provocative, joyful and celebrative of life and being. Specially the visual arts, classical music and dance. Love and lure of life and the world are embodied in the arts. My response to them resulted in a large number of poems. Also, I learnt to assemble visual images in poetry, resort to repetitions and resonances, to create rhythms and reverberations from them. Each collection of my poems, now fifteen of them, has carried poems about artists. I remain deeply grateful to the arts for revealing both reality and tremendous possibilities of the creative imagination.

Does poetry assume the role of conscience in our times? Can the arts also claim to be a site of conscience?

Joyce famously talked about 'forging the uncreated conscience of the race'. In some ways, this has been the task of literature across time. More so in ours, when most religions have chosen, unfortunately, to abadon and withdraw their roles as keepers of human conscience. Literature in our times has become the sole residence, the permanent address of conscience. The arts are also, by and large, sites of conscience. Altogether they resist the massive miniaturization of conscience being done by politics, science and religion in our times.

You once said that 'poetry is sufficient citizenship' and that a poet need not be active in civic or socio-political arenas. With your recent activism, have you undergone a change of heart or vision?

Writing is certainly a form of action, civic action. Normally it should be enough for a writer to write. But there are times when writing is not enough and some direct social action becomes imperative. In our times of growing intolerance, ethos of violence and murder, I, like so many other writers, hundreds of artists, scientists, film persons, felt outraged and have taken to direct protest, including return of national awards. This has drawn the attention of the larger public to a dangerous and devious trend. But let it be clear: we would be ultimately and truly judged by what we write, or paint or create. And those who have not taken to such protests are not necessarily less concerned about the assault on our pluralistic ethos and reality.

Many a time you've called yourself a shameless promoter of poetry. You think poetry needs this kind of promotion to survive in our times? Isn't all promotion harmful to creativity ultimately?

Poetry, as indeed all the arts, needs promotion, initiation, education. This is true across the ages. Unfortunately, in a climate of aggressive entertainment, glamorous noise and din, the still voice of poetry is being constantly pushed to the margins. It becomes necessary to promote poetry, respecting its autonomy and freedom, its plurality and complexity, its zeal for innovation. I've tried to do that by bringing to the notice of the public that poetry matters, that it speaks to them memorably and about our times and life, that it reveals to them realties which can only be discovered by and embodied in language. Such sensitive promotion hopefully escalates creativity; it cannot be harmful anyway.

You've organised many poetry events – from simple readings to Indian Poetry Festival, Asian Poetry Festival and World Poetry Festival. Do you believe that the quiet or aggressive voices of poetry should be heard by all through such fora?

Poetry emanates and appeals to all kinds of imagination, including the much-neglected auditory imagination. It is a verbal construct but also a voice. Hearing poems publicly recited by poets is always exciting. It reveals many unsuspected meanings and nuances. Hundreds and sometimes thousands of people have thronged these events, making it evident that they need poetry, it consoles and provokes them to new perceptions of life, reality, society, nature and self.

You've participated in many international poetry events. Tell us about some memorable experiences.

In Madeleine (Columbia) reading to thousands in a huge hall, in the open to hundreds in a workers' park and to a few hundred prisoners in jail have been the most memorable. Also, in Jerash (Jordan) in the Roman ruins; in Paris at a fair of poetry near St-Sulpice; in Lahore (Pakistan) to be told that 'Why do you call your language Hindi, it is Urdu as well!' in Dhaka (Bangladesh) to a packed hall reading in Hindi without Bengali translations and so on.

Translation has emerged as a major aspect of world poetry today. You've translated four major Polish poets into Hindi. You think translation has helped create a world audience/ readership for poetry, also its wider dissemination?

Translation is a major aspect of world literature now. In fact, the concept of world literature came into existence because of translation. But for translation many masters would have never reached and thrilled a worldwide readership. Translation has more or less created a worldwide community of writers as also of readers. Through translations we share many interests, anxieties and insights and in times of difficulty, censorship, restrictions, also solidarity and support. Poetry has certainly gained wider dissemination. Today we admire such masters as Yves Bonnefoy (French), Zbigniew Herbert (Polish), Adonis (Arabic), Shuntaro Tanikawa (Japanese), to name a few, through translations.

Your poetry has been translated into many Indian and foreign languages. Do you think justice has been done to your poetry? Or did it inevitably get 'lost in translation'?

Poetry has three possible lives: First, in itself, as the poet writes; second, in the readers, who read and respond to it and, third, when it is translated. Existing in another language, it cannot, and need not, be the same as in the original. There are many languages like Malayalam, Marathi, Gujarati, French, Polish, German, Russian, Spanish, Arabic in which I hear my poems: they sound strange and unrecognizable. They assume new lives and to see that happen is exhilarating! I believe in the axiom of Octavio Paz: poetry survives translation!

In your poetry, right from the beginning, there is an elegiac note, inspite of the tremendous and unmistakable zest for life. Why this somewhat tragic note which has grown more visible and audible in your later poetry?

I wish I knew the answer or a reasonable explanation! Sometimes I've explained it as an existential angst of a first child, lonely inevitably, of my parents. Sometimes by the fact that in my early childhood I was given up at least twice as dead. A deep sense of mortality falls like a shadow on a bright exuberant life. I cannot offer some religions explanation since I do not have the gift of belief.

You arranged your poems in four volumes: love, death and absence, home and ancestors, and the arts. The world, the arena of social strife, tension and turmoil is remarkably absent. Are you not concerned, as a poet, with what is happening in the social realm?

These books were selections on specific themes and there ought to have been at least two more volumes on 'The World' and 'The Others' which would have contained poems about our times, our social ethos, our difficulties with others. If you read the social in a simplistic way, I would perhaps be found to be lacking. But if you've a broader and complex view of the social, you may not be disappointed. Even a random list of images and phrases I've used would be enough to prove that I have not ignored or bypassed the social, that it is enacted and embodied in poetry through observation, exploration, evocation, resonance and memory. Besides, I have been quiet active socially about literature, poetry and the arts, and that is further evidence of my social concerns.

The world, its social dimensions are too complex: they can only be responded to in complex ways.

You once said that you were a poet of 'godless spirituality'. Would you please elaborate and also clarify as to how such a spirituality is relevant in a multi-religious society like India?

I believe that spirituality, at least for me, consists of the following elements: we are part of a cosmic reality and we not only live in the world and language, we also inhabit the universe. All things in the universe are interconnected and they are responsible for each other. Rivers, mountains, jungles, birds, animals have been quite responsible to humankind. But, sadly, humankind has not carried out its responsibility towards them in equal measure. We should refrain from 'othering' them and feel, deeply and always, that we are a large cosmic family. I also believe that poetry in our times could reinvent this spirituality. It cannot possibly be irrelevant to a multi-religious society like ours. It also does not need a god to head or supervise it!

You are widely known to be very interested and knowledgeable about world poetry. You've a large personal collection of books of world poetry in English translation. What do you think is happening today in world poetry?

Though major poets in the world today seem to be few and far, there is very rich and vibrant plurality of styles, approaches and idioms, visions and insights in world poetry. Mostly it is locally rooted, full of details which are personal, cultural, locational and yet it is poetry that speaks to us, makes us feel that in many languages, rhythms and crafts, we are all so touchingly, fortunately and imaginatively human and plural.

You started your career by being briefly a teacher of English literature, moved on to being a civil servant for about thirty-five years, became a cultural activist and a bold spokeman on behalf of Indian literature. Have these distinct phases of your life and career affected your poetic growth?

This is perhaps for others to say. Poets should not claim too much for themselves! Throughout all the phases of life and career I believe I've remained primarily and irretrievably a poet, looking at myself, my world and language, caught in love and lure of the world. Some earlier thematic concerns seem to have survived while others have withered away. Civil service made me see and feel reality at its most raw and perhaps poetry helped me humanise my civil duties and functions. I was always in some sense a cultural activist: it gets accentuated now. I have been deeply involved in the Indian literary scene and, once in a while, you have to be speaking boldly for it. I am sure that all these phases have made me understand myself, my poetry and its difficulties better. I may not have improved but I have persisted.

At 75 you are still writing poetry. And, of late, for the first time, you've attempted writing what could be called political poetry. Is this a new phase or just an interregnum?

It is true that until recently, until about a year-and-half ago, I did not write the so-called political poetry. Earlier I wrote poems about the Iraq war, Auschwitz, the demolition of the Babri Masjid etc. but they were not in a direct political idiom. When I felt that politics is moving towards a glittering but tyrannical mode, I wrote some direct poems. Finally they have to judged as poems, though, about politics. Politics keeps on interfering in our life, creativity, social relations so much – why shouldn't, once in awhile, poetry also interfere in politics? I do not know if this interference will continue.

With a vast repertoire of poets both from India and the world to choose from, which poets have influenced you?

All poets, barring geniuses, are stealers and apart from stealing from life and others, they often steal from other poets, especially the ancestors. I am no exception. I've stolen from so many that it is difficult even for me to recall all their names. Kalidas, Bhavbhuti, Kabir, Ghalib, Dev, Agyeya, Shamsher, Muktibodh, Raghuvir Sahay, Shrikant Varma. Also, Rilke, Eliot, Paz, Neruda, Herbert, Bonnefoy. I am so grateful to all of them that they have allowed me so readily to steal from them.

Have you never felt tempted to try some other, more popular, genres like fiction? Drama?

I have written a lot of prose, largely critical and memoirs, some in Hindi and some in English. But somehow I never felt tempted to try other creative genres. They require more sustained work and I am a needlessly busy person!

You gave the annual Poetry Society (India) lecture on 'Failure of Poetry'. Do you think you've failed as a poet or poetry, as such, has failed in our world?

I certainly may have failed in many ways. Inspite of many efforts, I do not think I succeeded in creating an enduring and expanding audience for poetry. I tried to bring poets and poetry into sunlight, as it were, for a while, but it did not last. My expectations from poetry have been too big. But failure of poetry is similar to that of Marx or Gandhi. A noble, tragic but grand failure.

Do you think the chasm between good poetry and popular poetry is unusually big in Hindi than in other languages?

Such a chasm has existed for long in almost all languages. Unfortunately, in Hindi this natural chasm has become unnaturally big due to several cultural and social factors. The Hindi belt suffers from cultural erosion, besides poor education. Together they have conspired to promote and expand poor taste for good poetry.

While you have many rhythms and their varieties in your poetry, you've hardly written in meters. You find metrical devices inadequate, inexact or what?

I think rhythm is the main thing in poetry. Meters are only well-devised and well-rehearsed structures of rhythm. I have tried many different rhythmic patterns but not strictly metrical forms. They are not necessarily inexact or imprecise but somehow I could not mould them to my poetic purposes. So I stopped even attempting. Maybe my poetic skill is not adequate to handle them competently and creatively. Many others have, successfully and significantly.

POETRY AS FICTION

By Ashok Vajpeyi

There are so many now who claim to possess the truth and then proceed to foist it upon others that it often feels as if were truth to be left alone it might perhaps survive, but now, close to the end of the century, it's hard to even say what truth is – is it a personal truth that emerges from the soul, or is it the blood-stained truth of cruelty, suppression and massacre? Perhaps the time has come for us to seriously consider that the extreme specialisations of science, the uniformity created by consumerist culture, philosophical problems and the limitless array of views and ideas make it not only impractical for literature to keep on being a claimant of truth, but that this is perhaps not even necessary for its existence or importance.

About sixty years ago, Einstein had said: 'As far as the laws of mathematics refer to reality, they are not certain, and as far as they are certain, they do not refer to reality.' The two main qualities of truth – of its being absolutely without expectation and of its being absolutely determined – were pretty much destroyed at the beginning of the century. Indeed, this century is unusual in that it has posed a challenge to all conceptions of truth, on the levels of both thought and action – to the extent that it has cast doubt upon whether there even is anything called truth, and whether it should exist. When the truth of science, the truth of philosophy, the truth of politics and religion wander like shadows through the corridors of this century, then it's hardly possible for the truth of literature and poetry to remain untouched or intact.

Saying this might seem like a devaluation of literature in human affairs. We who are writers and lovers of literature have held fast to the idea that literature is the primary medium for investigating and, ultimately, attaining truth. How can we so easily believe that it is no such thing, that it does not actually tell us the truth but tall tales about reality instead?

It isn't necessary here to repeat that poetry is a construct of language, that it hasn't descended from the heavens or the universe or from the sacred mouths of gods, that it is created or written by an individual in a language given him by society. The substance of language is the presence and activity of life and the material world. But is language merely an aggregation of life and the material world? This is not clear at all. It is our grasp on reality, it also gives us the opportunity to take part in and change it, and it expands itself in order to encompass new geographies of reality, often through the medium of literature. In it resides our memory, in it our dreams, and in it our imagination and courage. But isn't it, in some ultimate sense, the repository of our stories? In fact, all repositories of words – dictionaries – are really repositories of stories: an unending museum of the various images and things we make or find. Believing this does not make language fanciful or unreal, but instead moves it towards a more inclusive reality: we free ourselves from the opposition in logic, or the irreconcilable duality between truth and untruth, reality and dream.

Laying claim to truth is, in the end, a rejection of the ultimate mystery of the universe, whereas literature has for centuries been finding its life-source in that mystery. The simple and sincere acceptance of that mystery is possible in literature like it's possible nowhere else. In a world that is becoming more and more deprived of mystery, to accept it, to even conceive of it, is a radical thing.

While alienation from, tension with and separation from the past was one of the prime factors in the rise of modernism, there is in post-modernism, even if in an ironic way, the recognition of its own continuity, of its inseparability from the classical. Language is remembering once more, is dreaming, is creating instead of breaking. Poetry is discovering itself once more, is doubting itself once more – you might recall that Italo Calvino had advised politics to do the same. In fact, this is what has been happening in politics in the past couple of years: things have been changing so quickly that politics too is discovering and doubting itself.

Modernism has always been argumentative and, as Harold Rosenberg has said, always speaking for the present, whereas in post-modernism the present infiltrates the past.

Poetry is an imperfect art because language is an imperfect business. We can also say that human beings themselves are imperfect, even if they can imagine and sometimes discover perfection. Literature chooses this imperfection with all its complexity: to distill it into some broad generalisation or have it culminate in some truth is not the job nor the concern of literature or poetry. Poetry's concern, at most, is reality not truth. Reality which lives and functions with all its countless details and which cannot be assembled into any generalisation. In fact, the ethics of poetry mean that it should contain within it the realisation that the details with which it composes its reality are not the only ones and that countless other details exist besides. In the same way that other times exist besides its own time: both earlier and later. We don't go to poetry to search for or reach the truth, but to experience reality, to be part of it. Poetry does not proclaim the truth or research it: it sculpts its fiction from reality. That's why, as Borges has said, our memory, our imagination and our dreams are in it. It's not by chance that the reality of poetry (which is a reality it has discovered/found/created and is not separate from its particular form) resists being included in any other reality. We can feel some satisfaction, if we wish to, in noting the fact that the reality of literature is the only reality that does not try to colonise. It does not consider other realities to be inferior, or incomplete, and destined to merge with its own completeness. It's not necessary to go into this in detail because, living in this century, we all know very well how political, scientific and religious realities consider themselves complete and keep trying to colonise other realities. It would not be wrong to say that the lack of hesitation with which literature accepts the multiplicity of reality does not exist elsewhere: in this sense, literature is a stable democracy that has space for all realities and continuously resists any one reality's colonial or dictatorial attempts.

One way to think about it would be that religion, science, politics, etc. are all fictions created in order to understand, control, participate in and try to change reality – except that they all believe themselves to be concerned with truth. Only a poet can write, 'I write reality, and by writing it, I keep making it false.' That's why literature's enmity with simplification and generalisation is not just on the basis of differences in philosophy or strategy, but has a deeply ethical basis as well. It is cursed with reacting to the narrow breadth of generalisation or the non-inclusiveness of simplification because it doesn't consider itself or language to be the gist of reality – it isn't any sort of summation, nor does it want to be. It celebrates the multiplicity of the world: it is not a truth seeking generalisation, it is a fiction wandering in search of particulars and details. If the distance between prose and poetry – here in Hindi, and elsewhere in the world too – has reduced, if there is some intimacy and closeness in the languages of poetry and prose, it is not without reason: poetry has begun to understand that it is fiction.

Reality is delivered from another sort of fear in poetry, in that it doesn't need to erase or do away with any contradictions, or lapses in logic, or indecision or doubt. Literature doesn't try to avoid them. They remain, and because of them, the reality of literature remains unobstructed – in fact, in a sense, it attains its true verisimilitude. It can be said that neither literature nor democracy functions by suppressing or expelling their opposition: that's why totalitarian systems fear literature most of all. Because literature keeps alive the ideas of man's democratic existence and equal rights for all, even if it has to go underground. We should remember that what's happening in Europe, what's being called the democratisation of Europe, is being led from the front by writers and artists.

Poetry has usually been considered the opposition here. In a sense, it is indeed in permanent opposition to power. It constantly casts doubt upon power because it doubts itself with the same constancy. Truth can't doubt – only the fiction of reality can have the moral courage to doubt itself as much as it doubts others. Twentieth century literature can be legitimately interpreted as a narrative of constant doubt – about the word, about its power and authority, about its meaningfulness and its centrality. Which is something that, perhaps, can't be said of any other discipline. This doesn't make it any better than them, just different.

At this point it is necessary to recall that this century has seen terrible suppression and torture and war and massacre in the name of generalisations like revolution, nationalism, socialism, freedom, etc. All of these consider themselves to be indubitable and inarguable truths. But are we not today seeing the surprising sight of all these so-called truths turning out to be false and hollow? In this very century, hasn't some pretend-truth or half-truth become the ultimate truth by seizing power and gaining acceptance, hasn't it unseated the others mercilessly, and has it not – to its misfortune and our good fortune – in the end itself been unseated and reduced to dust? How laughable and pitiable they look now, those who made clear-cut divisions in the world, and made the cold war between those divisions the basis of modern thought and action?

Literature makes the decentralisation of the world its basis: it supports the democracy of multiplicity against the dictatorship of centrality. Maurice Blanchot said that, 'If you listen to your times you will find that they don't want you to speak on their behalf but to remain silent on their behalf.' Literature serves its purpose by refusing to remain silent. Because saying something directly often doesn't have a long-lasting effect, it says things indirectly. This obliqueness, this indirectness is what fiction is. It's also a way to make reality bearable. As Eliot said, humankind cannot bear very much reality.

There's also the aspect of transgressing limits. Literature is the expansion of language, it is also a continuous transgression of the limits that either it has set itself or those that have been imposed upon it by some external power. This includes transgressions of time and place, and of common moral behaviour – and of structure too, whether it's sentences or life-philosophies. A characteristic of this century's literature is that it's beauty emerges from transgression. If reality is a transgression of the determinate and simplified generalisations of truth, its totalitarian character, its harmony – then it is essential for poetry to be fiction in order to appropriate a reality beset by indecision, doubt, disorder, contradictions, etc. It is fiction, not truth, that can connect the finite to the infinite.

The French poet-critic, Yves Bonnefoy, has said that, 'Creativity lies not in writing but in giving a name to every thing and in listening to the mysteries of being that beat in it erratically.' He has further said, 'Words prove our nothingness, they open up a pit beneath us, but they can also give us the gift of a home.' Poetry encompasses both the void of nothingness and the fullness of home because it doesn't merely describe a situation but creates a presence. This presence is that space where, now and then, words become more than signs in an overflow of emotion, where words become things themselves. According to Bonnefoy, every poem nurtures a story in its heart. If we want, we can say that in this century at least, poetry has recognised with complete seriousness that it is an alternative: an alternative to truth, a fiction. Perhaps that's why Julia Kristeva has said, 'Experimental creations encourage the destabilisation of social systems.' And here Broch's saying also comes to mind: 'Science comforts, art disturbs.'

At a time when the word is being attacked from all directions, it is the fundamental duty of poetry to protect the word, its sanctity and dignity. All around us today is an immense misuse and exploitation of words. Whether it is the growing consumerism, or ideologies indifferent to and unaffected by intellectual developments and upheavals in the world, or newspapers working day and night in the service of sensationalism, or political and religious speeches making loud attacks on the scene – they are all tearing the word away from its meaning, its mystery, its polyphony, its internal resonances, the memories tied up within it, and are compelling it to become a medium merely for simple, direct communication. Disrespect for the word, boredom with its details, and carelessness with its use have become the permanent condition of our public life. Such is the situation that if you say something from a public platform, whether it's a newspaper or a religious or public congregation, no one will believe that you actually mean exactly what you say. Words have almost become unethical units: they're being used to draw the curtains upon hypocritical acts. Groaning under the weight of the immense simplifications of their time, but still undefeated, words can regain their fundamental ethical energy only in the twilight of fiction, in the corridors of the unexpected and the undetermined. To save the word, to keep it lit by its own light and the light of life, between imagination and reality, is not to be an aesthete but to save one of the greatest discoveries of humankind, to nurture its originality and its will to live. If words don't survive, humankind will also not survive, though immense truths and demonic machines might in a wordless, language-less desert. The survival of words is the survival of countless relationships and configurations of humankind and the world outside of it. Today, it's not just humankind's environment that is in danger, but its words as well. Whoever is ignorant of this danger has either already surrendered to the anti-human and anti-word forces, or lacks the courage to be a writer at the end of this century.

But how do words – at perhaps their lowest point in this horrible time – still survive? What is the source of their invincibility? If we look carefully, we will find that in those words that are still integral to the life of ordinary people, those that still carry some meaning, there is no deceit in their import or intention. Words don't draw the curtains on meaning, rather they illuminate it. These same words are also preserved in our old writings and classics in their full richness and creative plurality. In a way, tradition and ordinary life are what save words from complete defeat and meaninglessness, and keep alive the possibility of their becoming a polyphonic presence once again. Words are possibility in two senses: they are both product and thought.

Here in India we have, for the past century-and-half, started seeing literature in connection with social reality, its awareness of its time and of the destiny of humankind. To put it another way, its absolute contemporaneity is given primacy. In fact, in the context of literature, truth has come to mean realism, and the state and fate of time and humankind. If literature stays in the realm of mere fiction, then it's accused of having wandered away from these lofty goals and being reduced to wordplay. What creative imagination has given to the world, by straying away from hidebound ways and taking the path less trod, is self-evident. Take Hindi, where after Muktibodh's ideas of and experiments with fantasy, there can be no doubt that the reality and time of fiction are as true as that of any other medium that lays claims to truth. The courage to understand and fight for the destiny of humankind is the essence of the word, and it is impossible without imagination. By avoiding certainty, fiction makes itself believable: or, to borrow Milan Kundera's words, it refuses to be in service of predetermined truths. It is rooted not in mere factual accuracy, but in imagination and the fearless use of the intellect. In these new circumstances, if we remember Acharya Ramachandra Shukla's formulation, this is 'the free state of the heart released from the idea of its separate power'.

When it comes to poetry, human values inevitably get mentioned and it is a widely-held belief that poetry illustrates those values and in times of danger reaffirms and protects them. There isn't time to go into this in detail here, except to say that to protect language, with all its plurality, polyphony and internal resonances, and to protect the many points of view inhering in it, is also a value. It should not be forgotten that language is the everlasting symbol and source of our humanity and our ability to create values. It's indestructibility is the only insurance against the mortality of humankind.

Passing judgement on other disciplines like religion, politics, etc. from the platform of literature is not appropriate, although all these other disciplines never hesitate to pass judgment on literature. Literature challenges the right to pass judgement, challenges its ethicality even. Still, one must recognise that it isn't just poetry that is a fiction – every other discipline, no matter how all-encompassing or all-consuming, is also a kind of fiction: science is knowledge as fiction, politics is order as fiction, religion is philosophy as fiction. Whether they accept their fictiveness or not is, in this context, not our concern. We are only examining our position and our presence. The fictiveness of poetry does not mean an acceptance of its inferiority. But it does mean freedom from the ambition of being central, and freedom from the anxiety of not being central: you could say that poetry is indeed the extreme decentralisation of language. It is the search for a place that is its own, a place that refuses to be colonised by anything, not even truth. There is a destructive subtext to this, if one is looking for a metaphor for one's irrepressible pugnacity: it is a breach of the illusory fortress of truth.

By giving up its claim on truth, poetry frees up its own pure and unparalleled reality.

In conclusion, we are arguing for a plural vision, as opposed to the dictatorship of generalisation or simplification, as opposed to totalitarianism, and we are insisting on purity, on life-affirming complexity, on independence of thought and intellectual strength, on the primacy of the word, its creativity, on the primacy of life, on the protection of the linguistic environment and a recognition of its complex relationship to reality in poetry. If there exists a parliament of knowledge and reality, then we are making a case for a respectful and equal place for poetry in it. We are welcoming the transgression of the separation between life and art that has been thrust upon us.

Poetry as fiction is a difficult, life-affirming concept – it is choosing an immanent reality over a transcendent truth.

[One of three lectures delivered at Allahabad University as part of the Nirala Lecture Series in 1990.]

THE DOOR OF POETRY

By Ashok Vajpeyi

1.

About twenty-five years ago, I wrote a prose poem titled 'The Door':

The door could open. Not just when someone opened it but by itself too, because it wasn't fully closed. No one had closed it properly. Everyone is in a hurry to leave, not in a hurry to close doors properly. After we leave, the door is forgotten. If we didn't leave but stayed closed in or locked in there, then the door would remain – it's thought would remain. The door stops what's inside, and what's outside it stops from coming in. If there is no door, then what's closed in and what's locked out will get mixed up. Coming and going are effected through the door: but a little of the outside slips inside and a little of the inside slips outside anyway because the door is never fully closed. We forget to close it on purpose.

2.

If poetry is a door, then what does it close in, and what does it open to? Is it a few words, merely, and the few life experiences they illustrate? It knows that there are many things outside its bounds, things large and wide, which it can't encompass even if it wants. It knows that outside of whatever amount of life it can encompass, a much bigger and complex life still remains, with its countless ironies and contradictions and complexities. It knows that apart from the words that have come into it, there is a limitless treasure of words that it cannot make its own.

Poetry opens on to reality: it pulls into light the reality that has been lying inconspicuous or in the dark. It opens up an unknown part of it. Often it is under the illusion that it has grasped some essential truth about reality. But reality slips away from and outside of it, spreading far and wide. Reality's size and complexity imparts a lesson in humility to both the poet and to poetry.

Poetry opens on to language, and often that is where it flowers. Poetry isn't possible without language, but neither language nor poetry is possible without life. Poetry cannot believe that reality is only what has been put into words. While it's true that a lot of reality only becomes real once it comes into poetry or into language, but it's equally true that not all of reality comes into poetry, or even that it can. Every poem is a narrative of an incomplete reality.

3.

Poetry is not the only door: from a long time ago, human beings have searched for, found and opened many doors. Now the number of people has increased, and so has the number of doors. Poetry is a door that not many people use. There are many other doors more colourful and attractive, which you don't have to try too hard to open and which you can use to step into many colourful realties. The door of poetry is not easy to open: it requires some effort on your part. And then, often, it opens on to a reality that is not pleasant or entertaining. Most people don't have any interest in facing such realities. Poetry is a path to knowing others in oneself and oneself in others: those who would walk upon it were always rare, and it seems as if they are becoming rarer still.

4.

Poetry is not just a door, it is also a bastion. Perhaps the last bastion of the conscience in our time. Everything else – religion and science, politics and economics, management and the market, entertainment and broadcast media – has exiled the conscience. Many kinds of violence are becoming pervasive: the violence of terror and wars, the violence of rebellion and armed resistance, the violence in sport and cinema, the violence of electronic media, etc. Poetry resists violence, it shows people their blood-stained hands, it exposes the falsehood of innocent bloodletting: it strips away your pretence of being just a witness, and compels you to accept your complicity and responsibility. The door of poetry reveals the similarity between the rot in your backyard and the stench of your soul. It doesn't open on to any court of law, but to the court of our deeds.

5.

Poetry connects the individual to the community, and saves a place in the community for the individual. Individuality for it is both essential and extremely fertile, while its communality deepens its sense of responsibility. Poetry does not turn fiction into reality: but sometimes it changes reality into fiction.

6.

The majority of people are able to live happy and fulfilled lives without ever opening the door of poetry. Perhaps if they opened the door of poetry and peeked out from it, they might have seen or discovered something that they wouldn't have otherwise. Poetry can never believe that it is necessary.

7.

A good poem is written only rarely. By good I mean a poem whose door opens on to something unexpected and which reveals to us that such a wonder is possible in language.

8.

Poetry is obstinate because it refuses to be a disciple, because it tries its hardest to avoid being a follower of any thought or ideology, any philosophy or religion, any power or authority. It's true meaning can only be found through its form. It converses with all other disciplines, now and then it collaborates with them, sometimes it argues with and struggles against them, but it never gets disaffected towards or unseated from its own independent sensual domain.

9.

Now it feels as if the darkness is both spreading out and getting deeper. It also feels as if words are falling short. One way to test or judge a poem in our time might be to see which poems have – and in what manner and to what extent – recognised this deepening darkness, how much they respect it, and how far they have increased our vocabulary. This is the time to recognise the futility of attempting to go from darkness to some illusory light. This is the time to remember that the reduction of words is, in the end, a reduction of our humanity. A fundamental basis of our hold on reality is words: their reduction deprives us of many aspects of reality. Reality also searches for and discovers new words in poetry, and it brings alive those words that convey the pulse of reality in a deep and memorable way. The pulse and vitality of words is an expression of the flow of life.

10.

Poetry can't save us from fire and violence, from mortality and revenge, from hate and torture, from injustice and the market. But it can make us realise that these are not essential for the human condition and destiny, that it is we who have created and nurtured most of these, that it is we who are responsible for them. Poetry does not open a door from darkness to light. Through a small gesture, it makes us understand that we have the option of finding our way through the dark to the light. Poetry doesn't show the way, because most often it is searching for a way itself. What it does is invite you to become a part of this search.

11.

One must not expect too much from poetry, it's true. But it's equally true that we cannot ever completely despair of it. Poetry's place is somewhere between hope and despair. To pull it to any one side is to pull it away from its purpose. Our time is not the time of poetry because no time is the time of poetry. Poetry belongs to all times.

The Door of Poetry: From *Kavita Ke Teen Darwaze*, translated by Rahul Soni, 2016.

NOTES ON POETRY

By Ashok Vajpeyi

Poetry brings the poet close to the world: the poet may deny the world but poetry makes the world true for the poet. Many times the poet does not know that while making the world true, poetry also makes the poet true. Not free from the clutches of mortality, but neither now nor ever immortal.

That which every moment keeps slipping from our hands, like life or time, poetry, for a moment, seizes it. But for a moment only, since to aspire for more than that can lead to its own demolition.

Nowadays we struggle very little with time whereas it is destroying us every minute. And there are we under this illusion that we are saved and preserved only in time.

In the dark a little light seeps through the window as if hope leaving behind everything has come inside.

We hope in the dark. We do not ever have any hope from the dark.

For those who are able to believe in heaven and hell, who have lost all hope of immortality, who recognise the innate sadness of a voice, who see in falling leaves time itself withering, who know how to weep in silence, poetry is a spiritual haven. Only for them.

Always we are on some threshold or the other. Paths are nothing but distances between dream and reality: neither completely real nor only dream.

In literature those who know the goals already, often do not arrive at a destination. Only they reach it who meander and wander, who have no clue about the whereabouts of any destinations.

People come to poetry invariably late though poetry has time for them. Those alone who are able to stay with poetry for a while come to know that the time of poetry is without duration, interminable.

Poetry in the noon of mankind. It is neither prayer of the morning, nor the lament of the evening.

Poetry cannot be a rival of time. Poetry happens once in a while, as and when, but time keeps on happening all the while.

Poetry, remaining within limits, tries to touch and contain the limitless. It remains constantly self-conscious about its limits. In its attempt to touch the limitless, poetry does not turn limitless.

There should be no expectation from poetry. The meaning of a poem is beyond its expectation!

In poetry the sense that life is larger than poetry must never weaken – also that poetry cannot possibly contain the whole of life. But poetry, somehow and somewhere, prevents life from conclusion, postpones it, as also its passing away.

In the heart of the truth of poetry there is always a dream lurking. The truth of poetry is not possible without a dream outside poetry. Poetry simultaneously sees truth and dream one-into-the-other.

The world can carry on quite well without poetry, but poetry cannot do without the world. There is a world and hence there is poetry.

That which passes is time. That which is always against passing away is poetry.

Poetry is not possible without life, death, nature, love and word. It cannot be without objects either. Poetry is born out of wonder, mystery and attachment.

Only poetry could be open and luminous like day, dark and intense like night, hazy like dusk. The greed for things is always more alluring/tempting than the greed for words. Those who have words, sooner or later, are able to acquire things as well. But those who have lots of things, invariably, feel short of words!

Surrounded, as we are, by the cosmic, poetry could only be reluctance or stammering. After all, in which of us, the cosmos speaks?

FAILURE OF POETRY

By Ashok Vajpeyi

I used to believe, quite frankly, and I still partly do not disbelieve, that I am most human in my own way when I am with poetry, whether writing or reading it. And yet, it seems that what has happened must be taken into account. I only hope that sharply critical as my remarks are to follow, they are not only born out of exaggeration and prejudice, which are two salient features of whatever I do. They are also born out of pain and hurt and though I am a laughing person, a smiling person, I smile all the time, I smile mostly out of pain. Why should one inflict one's pain and suffering on others? So I keep on smiling. I remember a Jewish proverb: 'Weep before god, laugh before man'. I discovered easily in life that I don't have a god to weep before, so I decided to laugh before man. More than laughing at others, laugh at yourself! At least I commit many mistakes, stupidities, on a daily basis. There is enough material for me to laugh at myself. In a way poetry became and continues to be my god, a god that failed!

Now as you look at the map of world poetry (if there could be a map of world poetry) it would appear as if these are not the times for great poetry. When the twentieth century started you had such great figures like Rainer Maria Rilke, Rabindranath Tagore, Eliot and Yeats. As you come to the twenty-first century, I think you can count the truly great poets on a single hand and perhaps there are not even fifteen of them! Yves Bonnefoy in France, the Arab poet Adonis, Tanikawa Shintaro, a Japanese poet. They are very few and it is not that we don't know enough. Translation has become a major affair and you know more or less great poets across the world, across the languages.

There is a lot of poetry. There are minor poets, mediocre poets, and a majority of third-rate poets, popular poets, and suchlike. Even in India you can imagine many popular poets who are not exactly good poets and a very large number of minor poets who enjoy huge popularity. Good poets are far and few. I would cite a quotation of the great Polish poet Zbigniew Herbert who said, 'History does not know a single example of art or an artist anywhere ever exerting a direct influence on the world's destiny – and from this sad truth follows the conclusion that we should be modest, conscious of our limited role and strength.' Quite contrary to the advice given by him, what I am going to say is born out of huge expectations from poetry. I am not willing to accept a modest role. It was Joseph Brodsky who said that the poet must be like a stone and should hit hard. If he didn't have the courage to do so, he should stop writing poetry and do something else. What I am going to say really is born out of great expectations from poetry, a great trust in the capacity of poetry to be able to do that and the failure of poetry to do so. Famously, W.H. Auden said in his great poem about the death of W.B. Yeats, 'Poetry makes nothing happen.' In the twentieth century itself, poetry was called to action on many fronts, invited to accompany social action resolutions, and yet here was one of the major poets saying poetry makes nothing happen! You look at what Milosz, the Polish poet who also became a Nobel Laureate, said, 'If we look at this century, an extremely small part of human experience has been fixed in language and literature'. We may wonder how small a percentage of what mankind has lived remains in their languages. We could as well ponder as to how small a percentage of what man has gone through in the twentieth century has gone into language, which produced great poetry and great literature! Newton called poetry 'this ingenious nonsense'. I am reminded of an episode when one of the great poets of Hindi, 'Nirala', was staying with another major poet of Hindi, Makhanlal Chaturvedi. The gardener was working around and Nirala walked upto him and started talking about his family. Though he had three sons, he said that he was blessed with only two sons – the third son wrote poetry, being good for nothing. You are not counted as a social being in the social milieu if you are a poet.

Poetry, in any case, is a minority activity in most languages in terms of its writers and readers. In fact, I don't know but I suspect that there is a slowing down of poetry-writing in most languages: many more people are drawn to fiction. Fiction brings money, fame, poetry brings almost nothing. Most poets are unsuccessful in making a living by writing poetry alone. Keki Daruwalla, in the civil service, myself in the civil service, we could not live by poetry alone. Nowhere in the world, poets could earn enough to live a decent life unless there were fellowships , honorary professorships, reading sessions and all that. Most people seem to live life happily without poetry. I live in a housing society and they know that I am a poet, but out of the five hundred residents, no one has ever come to me to ask what kind of poetry I write! They are just not interested in the fact that I am a poet. When I describe myself as a poet, I conceal the fact that I was a civil servant. And by that I am reduced to nothing. It is quite interesting to watch how most people, unless they have to read poetry, suffer poetry! Textbooks are taught very badly, very uninspiringly, very damaging in fact to any poetic sense that might survive in you. And if you become a poet in spite of your education, it can't be because of your education, rather you must have taken some stupid decision in spite of your education. Through centuries, states and governments, and even philosophers, have looked at poetry and poets with great suspicion, and the great philosopher Plato, with whom Western civilisation started, wanted the poets out of the republic. They were not desirable there. And then, in this world dominated by media, glamour, there is very little, almost no, presence of poetry. What is present there in terms of slogans, may be some advertisement line, 'Umeed ka rang tumhare sang', that's not poetry. What are the implications of this situation? The implication quite simply is: poetry fails to inspire people at large. It just doesn't interest them. That's why they are not there. They are inspired by other things. You may think that people ought to have better tastes, that they ought to enjoy good poetry, but the fact remains that people at large just don't enjoy it. We live in a world which is very complex and very confusing in many ways. It is not one world but several worlds rolled into one perhaps.

One of the jobs of poetry has been to re-imagine the world for us and sadly that doesn't happen any more. Maybe it is being re-imagined by other disciplines more effectively, more directly. Poetry is not able to create concern and respect for either plurality or equality or indeed language. Poetry, at one level, is one of the only possible democracies. The republic of imagination in which everything is equal, and things are not reduced to or simplified in some single categories. There are enormous numbers of pluralities that poetry handles or is supposed to address and there are enormous ideas, characters, persons and objects which are given equal status, as it were, in the republic of poetry. Yet, in spite of this, poetry is not able to create a deep sense of plurality or a deep sense of equality or even a deep sense of language. After all poetry is an activity in language, it is an action of language. According to Paul Valéry: 'it is a beautiful accident of language'. Even if it is beautiful, it is an accident, but in language, poetry ought to inspire some curiosity, some deep resources in your psyche which could be linguistically animated. This does not happen. It has not succeeded in forging and establishing what I call the other republic of imagination, the other reality. T.S. Eliot famously once observed that one of the jobs of poetry is to preserve the purity of the language of the tribe, purity not in the sense of grammatical correctness or verbal exactitude but a certain core of the language. I don't think that this preservation of the language of the tribe has been achieved by poetry. Language is being dismantled, distorted, used carelessly, used mindlessly all along and there is no way in which poetry can possibly bring sense even to some, a minority that would listen to the voice of poetry. Language is something worthwhile. Language is worthwhile preserving. Poetry is no longer generally of any social use. If you look at the proceedings of the Indian Parliament, which has a good reflection of what is happening in this so-called socio-political world in which we live, once in a while poems are quoted. But they are rather dated. They are not even the best poems of those poets who have composed the quoted lines and they, in any case, come from a period which is actually fifty-sixty years old. No single poem, recently written, has ever found mention, much less reading, by any parliamentarian! So, it has no social use. It can't even be used in a budget speech. When Mr Chidambaram gives a budget speech, he quotes an Alvar poet. It is like me mentioning Kabir. Of course, there has been great poetry before, and sometimes I suspect that poetry has watched helplessly the hold and meaning of reality snatched from itself by prose, by other means. So poetry doesn't have as much a hold on reality. It has been taken over by others who are doing it much better. They have more direct access to reality. Even reality seems to be slipping in a way. It has not been able to respond to the new aspirations and anxieties of the youth as manifested in popular music, in bands, in the visual arts, in design, etc. Young people want creative expression and poetry is not one of the means they resort to. They express themselves through other means. As poets, we have ceased to say anything significant to these young people.

I am indulging in exaggeration and deep prejudice. There was a time when poetry was the avant-garde, it was in the forefront. You can think of any number of movements which were started in poetry and some of them later went over to other disciplines from poetry. I don't think that the role of the avant-garde is any longer being played by poetry. There are many avant-garde expressions of different kinds, but poetry is, sadly, not one of them.

One of the objectives of poetry was to retain, to reanimate, to rehabilitate racial memory. The memory of the society, the social memory, and that role also seems to have been given up. There is very little poetry which will resonate with racial memory. There is very little poetry which will hark back to something you should remember and not forget. We live nowadays in a permanent present. We have been thrown into this permanent present, and there is a massive amnesia as if nothing has happened before, as if nothing has existed before, as if no poetry has been written before. We are the first ones, even those minor ones think so who come first time on the stage. Therefore, there is this very essential function, the memory function, the social memory function, poetry has more or less given up. Now poetry no longer gives us new mythical structures, new symbols with which contemporary man could identify (you can remember any number of symbols, images and utterances from the twentieth century which were given to us by the poets) to describe reality, to describe our times. We just don't have them from poetry anymore. We can't think of even one telling line. I am talking of the global scene. I am not talking only of India. This is the scene all over.

One of the roles of poetry was to offer resistance to the status quo. At least moral resistance, if not other kinds of resistance. There were occasions when political resistance was also offered by the poets. But at least a moral resistance, that urge to resist, such as the urge to break which created the avant-garde, also seems to be on the way out. I think poetry is no longer able to cope with the world now dominated by poverty and exploitation or opulence in plentitude, fashion, glamour, etc. There is no middle space which is being either discovered by poetry or addressed by it. As if at the extremities of poverty and deprivation, or of opulence and plentitude, poetry is not able to look either way or to discover or address the middle space, if there is any. I have said it before, but let me put it in different words: Poetry does not seem to aspire to create an alternative world of complexities, activities, depth and resonance. It is no longer bothered about expanding and deepening a sense of language amongst us. The responsible, refined and civilised, actually civilised dialogue, civilised conversation, seem to have become a very rare phenomenon. Either abuse each other, scream at each other, shout at each other, on TV, in parliament, on the streets. We Indians are the noisiest people in the world anyway. There is no civilised conversation left where people can disagree, hugely, with each other and yet speak. And one of the functions of literature, and for that matter of poetry, was to civilise our speech. The child speaking his or her mother tongue is complimented these days! The decline of this civilised speech, even of the mother tongue, has something to do with the decline of poetry. I have to assume that poetry has failed to perform that role also.

There is only one poet in Hindi, Vishnu Khare, who writes on cricket. How many poems are there about cricket, hockey, football? These are the areas which demand poetic address. It was said in the West that poetry must delight and instruct. Poetry today neither delights nor instructs; I am at a loss to know what it does. Instructive not in a dialectic manner but in a deep, moral way. Unfortunately, and despite the problem all along, somehow bad, sentimental and banal poetry has become rather popular and successful. In Hindi there is a very clear division between good poetry and popular poetry. Sentimental or humorous poetry: no one takes it seriously, but thousands of people listen to it with much delight. It is such a saddening fact. And there is very good poetry lying in books, in the hearts of these poets, ageing – some of them – but nothing improves. So there is a very deep divide between the popular and the significant poetry. It was not so earlier, the hiatus seems to have widened. And therefore, poetry speaks only to the initiates, it has become a kind of a courtly activity, most poets speak to other poets, most of us over here are either poets or going-to-be poets or hidden poets or aspiring poets, or failed poets like me. But we are poets and, therefore, we are interested in the fate of poetry. Nobody else is interested. Therefore we have come out of courtesy, a minority activity more or less. In fact we are a minority, whether we realise it or not; we seem to be living in a ghetto of our own making. There is a poetry ghetto in which we are now caught, wherein we give a moral boost to each other to keep the morale high but we know we are doomed and that we are within the confines of a ghetto. The ghetto will sooner or later be destroyed, if not bombed out of existence.

And then poetry today lacks 'new architecture', in keeping with the vast mind-boggling changes societies, words of communication, languages are going through. We need a different kind of poetry, a new poetics. If there is a need for new architecture in all kinds of other things, why not such a need in poetry is being felt? The world is becoming more complex, structurally more intense. There was a different time and you remember again what Czeslaw Milosz called in his Nobel acceptance lecture 'The Witness of Poetry'. Another Nobel Laureate, Seamus Heaney, called it 'The Redress of Poetry'. It was much talked about how poetry in the twentieth century has been witness. Are we, the poets, really the witness today of what is happening? Is this poetry witness of what is happening to all, whether individually, or socially or morally? I suggest not. We have given up even that role, much less participating in what is happening, we are not even witnessing ... *hum Ram jharokhe se bhi nahi daikh rahe, humne jharokha bund kar rakha hai* ... we seem to be caught in this. You could recall that Mathew Arnold at the end of the nineteenth century predicted that religion will be replaced by poetry. This was, of course, a high hope. Nothing of that kind happened, but what did happen is that most religions have abandoned or betrayed their inherent spirituality. Most religions today are aggressive, intolerant, completely devoid of spirituality. Perhaps poetry could have been the new residence of spirituality. By spirituality I don't mean spirituality in the conventional sense, but spirituality in the sense of being part of a larger reality, being responsible for each other, feeling that the world is not only made up of human beings but also of other beings including even inanimate forms, and that we are responsible for all this. This is spirituality that we can share with each other in many ways. All this seems to have been given a go-by. Spirituality was abandoned by religions and didn't find a new residence in poetry. So it floats, sort of unlocated, homeless in some sense.

I think poetry no longer creates love and lure of the world, and poetry is born out of the love of the world. As a poet you love the world, not that you are satisfied with the world, not that you don't think of an alternative world, but you think of an alternative world because you love the world. But I don't think that this love and lure of the world are any longer the motive of poetry. Poetry does not inspire because you have to love the world not generally, you have to love the world in detail, in images, in specifics. That kind of love and lure that ought to be created by poetry do not seem to be happening. I sometimes suspect that many humanly-created discovered/sustained rhythms and structures are on the verge of extinction. One of the jobs of poetry was to keep animating that which is created by man and which is likely to be lost. There are any number of rhythms, structures, metrical and non-metrical devices which are just getting lost and beyond retrieval. They will only exist in old texts.

I have marvelled at the fact that there are one lakh words in my language, Hindi. This means that there are one lakh ways of naming, participating, describing, narrating, exploring, perhaps changing reality in my language. One lakh devices, but how many of them are used in normal parlance? Perhaps 2,000-3,000. In media, it will be around 5,000, in poetry unfortunately around 10,000! So even the linguistic resources that you have are so inadequately exploited by the contemporary poetic imagination. Words live not in dictionaries, they live in created texts which animate them, bring them to life. But if they are not fully allowed to remain there, ultimately they will be extinct, they will die out, and I think this is what is happening: words are dying and poetry is listlessly watching! Our verbal resources in poetry are being depleted fast as never before. There are fewer words with which poetry is being written at least in some of the Indian languages. Its intellectual rigor is missing and moral authority also seems to be getting lost. Adam Zagajewski, another Polish poet, wanted in poetry discovery of new forms of evil, new varieties of good, new forms of behaviour and ageless ways of life. They are all more or less adjourned. We are not looking at new forms of evil, new varieties of good, whatever.

Lastly, poetry has lost what I call the epic impulse. That is, the impulse to cover a wide range of reality. We have become so lyrical and we feel so happy with the lyrical because we can manage it much better. And the epic imagination requires grappling with reality, ideas, objects, characters, narratives, etc. At least in the

Indian languages in the last almost forty years, no epic of any consequence has been written, not even a long poem like 'The Wasteland', (T.S. Eliot) or 'Andhere Me' (G.M. Mukhtibodh), for instance, which had epical ambitions. And we, who had the great tradition of epics – in fact, Indian civilisation can be said to be born after two great epics, the Ramayana and the Mahabharata. But in the last fifty years, there has been no harking back to these epical traditions. They have become irrelevant to our creative memory and endeavour, as it were. I don't remember anything written like 'Andha Yug', 'Sriradha' and 'Asadhya Veena'. The epic impulse we have handed over to the novel, the epic saga, that kind of writing has gone over to prose from poetry. If you don't have the epical impulse, you are like some infant collecting pebbles on the sea shore when the sea is roaring. That's what the world is. It is the sea roaring, and we are collecting pebbles on the shore. That is quite an innocent way: touching things which cannot sustain you for long. Pebbles are not going to make you fit to face the fury of the sea. But then, this sense of the failure of poetry that I have described to you is born out of a deep expectation from poetry. I almost seem to be suggesting that if poetry cannot be great, it is not worth it. Now one can say that everybody can't be a great poet. Nobody will stop writing poetry just because he had heard my lecture! Everybody is going to try their hand in new ways and nobody can stop anybody from being a good or bad poet anyway. So that's not the intention, but the point is that in this world, which is full of lust and greed, full of violence and violations, excesses and disruptions, money and markets, prices and auctions, poetry is hugely irrelevant: a failed enterprise. But perhaps, in its failure there is the only moral dignity possible to language. We have not succumbed, we may have failed in performing our tasks competently, imaginatively, but we have not succumbed to the material and moral temptations of the age, to greed and lust. There is some moral dignity, therefore, in this failure. It is much better perhaps to fail in this world than to succeed in it.

This is a modified version of the annual lecture delivered at the Poetry Society of India in 2014.

AFTERWORD

Ranjit Hoskote

Most poets conceal themselves beneath the camouflage of a professional identity, wearing the badge of a respectable occupation, giving themselves titles that require no further explanation or justification, and speaking the language of a trade that is socially acknowledged as useful. Not, indeed, because we are ashamed of what we do – quite the contrary – but because such a strategy gives us the necessary freedom and space in which to pursue our secret, our real lives, the lives we lead as artisans dedicated to a continuous and productive struggle with language, as citizens of the republic of the imagination. Whatever the nature of the host culture that has offered convenient accommodation to the poet in the world of everyday activities – the newspaper office, the civil service, the insurance company, the publishing firm, the advertising agency – the interiority of poetic practice continues to flourish beneath the surface of outward commitments, asserting itself despite the claims made on the poet's time and energies.

So far, so Manichean. What complicates this simple duality between the manifest and the secret life is the danger that one might become as involved in the quest for experiment and excellence in one's outward career as in one's interior practice. This, in my reading, is the challenge with which Ashok Vajpeyi has had to wrestle over many decades; certainly throughout the course of his career as a distinguished civil servant, from 1965 to 2001, when he contributed in seminal and abiding ways to postcolonial Indian culture as a cultural administrator and institution-builder. Asserting that the poet's pilgrimage is nurtured rather than slowed down by the drudgery of quotidian work, Vajpeyi has written: 'Poetry enters heaven with mud-soaked shoes.' Fortunately, he was able to transfigure his quotidian work through the prism of culture: he was instrumental in the foundation or transformation of several cultural institutions, most memorably Bharat Bhavan in Bhopal, an institution that hosted a grand confluence of poetry, the visual arts, theatre, cinema, architecture and research during his tenure there. The figures he brought together to animate Bharat Bhavan included the painter J. Swaminathan, the poet and fiction-writer Dilip Chitre, and the theatre director B.V. Karanth. The building that houses Bharat Bhavan is no standard-issue PWD construction either; it was designed by the celebrated architect, Charles Correa. There, also, Vajpeyi convened an international biennale of poetry as well as an international biennale of the graphic arts; under Swaminathan's tutelage, a museum of contemporary art by metropolitan as well as rural artists was established. Eventually, and having survived various political vicissitudes, Vajpeyi concluded his career as culture secretary to the Government of India; after his retirement, he has continued to be active in the cultural sphere and has, among other mandates, served as chairman of the Lalit Kala Akademi, India's National Academy of the Fine Arts.

Throughout these busy years as a cultural catalyst and convenor, Vajpeyi has maintained a consistent and acclaimed record of literary production, as a poet, critic and essayist whose affective and intellectual investments span the arts. A long period of relative publishing silence had followed his first book of poems, *Shahar Ab Bhi Sambhavana Hai* (1966); he made up for this with a surge of volumes during the 1980s and 1990s, including *Ek Patang Anant Mein* (1984), *Agar Itne Se* (1986), *Tatpurush* (1989) and *Kahin Nahin Wahin* (1991). Over the last five decades, he has founded and edited journals, and written literary criticism. His criticism has proceeded, not from a desire to demarcate the vanquished and the triumphant in the cycles of avant-garde warfare, but to praise the writers he loves and to share his enthusiasm for them with others. Meanwhile, his writings have been translated into German, Spanish, French, Russian, Polish, Hungarian, Arabic, Norwegian, and – until this substantial translation by Rahul Soni – somewhat sporadically into English. Among Vajpeyi's most moving testaments, both in poetry and prose, are his acts of homage to the music of Kumar Gandharva and the paintings of S.H. Raza.

Never shy of embracing classical visions of the cosmos, even as he has contested the claims of those conservatives who would narrow and ossify an originally vibrant and mercurial tradition into a repository of crude prohibitions and inhibitions, Vajpeyi invites his readers, in the course of an interview he once gave, to consider an expansion of the Sanskrit model of the pancha-maha-bhuta. 'The classical Indian view has been that the universe was created out of five elements – earth, water, fire, ether and wind. I add language as the sixth element that makes earth a world for us. Language, together with god, time and abstraction are four radical inventions of Homo sapiens.' If language is one of the six great elements that form the substance of the universe, and therefore one of the great and universally available resources for human sustenance, we have been entrusted with a demanding and magnificent responsibility. Just as we might poison and degrade earth, water, fire, ether and wind with our toxic activities and our dangerous negligence towards the ecology, so too might we poison and degrade language. The poet takes, as her or his mandate, the resistance to such a destruction of language. It takes the poet from solitude to sociality, from the intimate relationship with the word and the page to a more public relationship with those who use, misuse, abuse and sometimes are transported by words.

I picture Vajpeyi as he spent the years of his career as a civil servant: he sits at the large glass-topped table that serves the senior member of the Indian Administrative Service as a command post; he sits in a padded chair with a towel draped over the back, the legacy of British administrators coping with the heat and dust of the tropics and the exhaustion of punkah-wallahs. He listens all day to colleagues who speak the argot of Indian bureaucratese. Curtailing his irrepressible sense of humour, he reads their submissions and memoranda without laughing at their needfuls and their expedites, their herewiths and their therewiths. He goes through the usual relay of files, making the marginal 'notings' that are necessary, retaining for the telephone those remarks that are best not recorded in writing for posterity. And all the while, his mind continues to crackle with distant yet visceral electricities: if he is reading Muktibodh, Agyeya, Shrikant Verma, Shamsher Bahadur Singh, Arun Kolatkar, he is also reading Czeslaw Milosz, Zbigniew Herbert, Miroslav Holub, Nazim Hikmet and Eugenio Montale. He is making plans for poetry festivals and platforms that can host dialogues among the arts. He is working on collaborations among the adjacent yet estranged, such as metropolitan modern artists and rural folk artists; he is dreaming of startling encounters among dissimilar practitioners, from South-east Asia, East Europe, South America, and from across India's spectrum of regions, languages and ideologies.

*

Ashok Vajpeyi was born in 1941 in the city of Durg, then in the Central Provinces and Berar, and now in the state of Chattisgarh. He grew up in the university town of Sagar, then in the Central Provinces, later in Madhya Bharat, and now in Madhya Pradesh. Sagar boasts the oldest university in Madhya Pradesh. The definition of the territory around it may have changed, but the town has retained its special character; and for those who grew up there and were nourished by its academic and intellectual ethos, such as Vajpeyi, it holds a special significance. Like Hubli-Dharwar, Miraj, Jhansi, Allahabad, Shimla and Cuttack, Sagar was a node in that cartography of university towns, railway junction towns, district headquarters, cantonments, hill stations and pre-jet travel international refuelling stops which today we too easily relegate to the forgotten domain of the provincial. In actuality, these non-metropolitan, so-called mofussil zones were alive with their own distinctive cosmopolitanisms, their gift for melding a proximate and dynamic culture with the distant elsewheres of international modernity. Vajpeyi carried the impulses of Sagar with him to New Delhi, where he studied at the prestigious St. Stephen's College, and eventually both into the civil service and into his poetry. Thinking of the sublime vocalist and denizen of Dharwar, Mallikarjun Mansur, whose music he greatly admires, Vajpeyi memorialises him in a manner that evokes the deceptive backwardness and the confident sophistication of the supposedly provincial (the adroit translation is Rahul Soni's):

> Setting his own pace
> Mallikarjun Mansur
> comes in
> late
> and marches ahead of time

I have always been fascinated by Vajpeyi's breadth of references, and by his ability to frame these into a kaleidoscope of differential patterns in his poetry. Like all sensible artists – I say this as one whose somewhat schizoid fate it is to be both a poet and a theorist – he dispenses with the constricting territorial conceptions of ideologues and the Procrustean periodisations of scholarly specialists. Instead, he embraces a transregional and transhistorical approach that is festive in its declaration of affinities with the proximate and the distant, the inherited and the contemporary. In his poetry, we sense the presence of Kabir just as much as we sense the astringent presence of the samizdat poets of the Soviet Union and the Warsaw Pact countries, the lavish opulence of the poets of Latin America. If he became familiar with the former through oral and the scribal cultures of transmission, he became acquainted with the latter through the Penguin Modern Poetry in translation series that Ted Hughes and Daniel Weissbort had edited and sustained, and which he read during the 1970s.

Vajpeyi's education in sensibility has been diverse and multifaceted; his lifelong friendships and fascinations with musicians and dancers has also brought into his poetry a nimble awareness of temporality and cadence. It is not the phantoms of a congealed tradition that matter to him, nor is it a regional identity that defines him; rather, he defines himself through the self-consciously mapped and secured position of the dissenter, even the dissident, whose sense of a personal choice and destiny rescues him from becoming the spokesperson of an ideology, a nation-state or a public cause. Which is not to say that Vajpeyi turns his back on the urgencies that exercise all of us as members of a body politic, of a society caught up in the turbulence of multiple and vexed transitions, out of the colonial and into the global. On the contrary, he is fully engaged with the crises of aggressive populism, ascendant majoritarianism, incipient authoritarianism, and the exactions they make upon the freedom of individuals, the solidarity among communities, and the liberality of the public sphere. Vajpeyi's understanding of the global contemporary would accord well with the sociologist Zygmunt Bauman's account, we experience the meltdown of identity and location that the 'liquid modernity' of globalisation orchestrates while also suffering the 'neo-tribalisms' that such a meltdown unleashes in reaction.

Meditating on the cycles of violence that have attended the rise of a politicised religiosity in India, and dwelling on such cataclysmic moments as the destruction of the Babri Masjid in Ayodhya by Hindu-majoritarian militants in 1992, the bomb attacks in Bombay in 1993, and the systematic ethnic cleansing of the Muslim minority in Gujarat in 2002, Vajpeyi wonders where such brutality leaves language and the practitioners of the linguistic arts:

> A rotting, burning stench emanates from language –
> it's coated in blood and rags and brutally broken bones:
> prayer has turned into a terrible curse
> neighbourhoods are places of murder, streets are galleries
> of violence
> those who were our own until yesterday have been
> othered today:
> there are no bloodstains on the murderers' faces but the
> aura of victory
> I watch helpless at how words are sullied,
> how hate is woven into the structure of language,
> how the neighbourhood is cast out of poetry.

Can the forms and resources of language and of poetry be retrieved from the horrors of hate speech, from the barbarity of propaganda, from the flattening and nullifying impact of slogans? Might a certain degree of abstraction, seemingly a search for purity of form but equally a search for new and as-yet unnamed idioms of sensuous delight, act as a resolution to the problem of a violated language? Might the extension of the intellect and the senses into domains beyond the discursive help to renew language, to offer it fresh bibliographies of sensation? In a poem dedicated to the painter Raza, a close friend of many decades now, on his eightieth birthday, Vajpeyi celebrates the variability of the artistic quest, the shifting relationship of power between the self and time, the form achieved through effort and the elusive significance of which the form is a herald and approximation:

Time isn't a stone building surrounded by trees and shrubs:
sometimes you lay out paper on the heavy stone table inside,
sometimes your desires,
sometimes all the sadness you have collected in your life,
but you can't live in it

because you live in indelible colours,
in their luminosities,
in the darknesses pulsing between their layers.

It is in the luminosities and the darknesses pulsing between Ashok Vajpeyi's lines that we find sources of replenishment. They speak to us of the world of asymmetries and anxieties in which we live, but also point to continents of hope and dream yet to be charted.

Bombay, January 2016

Ashok Vajpeyi is a Hindi poet-critic with fifteen books of Hindi poetry to his credit. He has published many volumes of criticism, in both Hindi and English, on poetry, literature, the visual arts and Indian classical music. Book-length translations of his poetry have appeared in French, Polish, German, English, Bengali, Marathi, Odiya, Gujarati, Urdu and Rajasthani. A recipient of the Sahitya Akademi Award (1994), Dayavati Kavi Shekhar Samman (1994) and Kabir Samman (2006), he has also been decorated by the President of the Republic of Poland with the outstanding national award 'The Officer's Cross of Merit of the Republic of Poland' (2004), and by the French government with the award of 'Officier De L'Ordre Des Arts Et Des Lettres' (2005). A major institution-builder and a cultural activist, he lives in Delhi after retiring from the civil service.

Rahul Soni is a writer, editor and translator. His translations include Pankaj Kapur's novella, *Dopehri*, Shrikant Verma's Sahitya Akademi Award-winning poetry collection, *Magadh*, and International Booker Prize winner Geetanjali Shree's acclaimed novel, *The Roof beneath Their Feet*.

HARPERPERENNIAL

Harper Perennial presents special editions of its finest books in translation

Apradhini
Shivani
Translated from the Hindi by Ira Pande

Avasthe
U.R. Ananthamurthy
Translated from the Kannada by Narayan Hegde

Blue Is Like Blue
Vinod Kumar Shukla
Translated from the Hindi by Arvind Krishna Mehrotra and Sara Rai

Diary of a Malayali Madman
N. Prabhakaran
Translated from the Malayalam by Jayasree Kalathil

Farewell, Mahatma
Devibharathi
Translated from the Tamil by N. Kalyan Raman

The Golden Gandhi Statue from America
Subimal Misra
Translated from the Bengali by V. Ramaswamy

A Name for Every Leaf
Ashok Vajpeyi
Translated from the Hindi by Rahul Soni

Moustache
S. Hareesh
Translated from the Malayalam by Jayasree Kalathil

Seven Sixes Are Forty-Three
Kiran Nagarkar
Translated from the Marathi by Shubha Slee

Shameless
Taslima Nasreen
Translated from the Bengali by Arunava Sinha

HARPERPERENNIAL

Age of Frenzy
Mahabaleshwar Sail
Translated from the Konkani by Vidya Pai

A Life Incomplete
Nanak Singh
Translated from the Punjabi by Navdeep Suri

Mohanaswamy
Vasudhendra
Translated from the Kannada by Rashmi Terdal

The Music of Solitude
Krishna Sobti
Translated from the Hindi by Vasudha Dalmia

No Presents Please
Jayant Kaikini
Translated from the Kannada by Tejaswini Niranjana

A Preface to Man
Subhash Chandran
Translated from the Malayalam by Fathima E.V.

The Secret Garland
Andal
Translated from the Tamil by Archana Venkatesan

Shala
Milind Bokil
Translated from the Marathi by Vikrant Pande

The Weary Generations
Abdullah Hussein
Translated from the Urdu by the author

Written in Tears
Arupa Patangia Kalita
Translated from the Assamese by Ranjita Biswas

HARPERPERENNIAL

Bhima
M.T. Vasudevan Nair
Translated from the Malayalam by Gita Krishnankutty

Chemmeen
Thakazhi Sivasankara Pillai
Translated from the Malayalam by Anita Nair

Ghachar Ghochar
Vivek Shanbhag
Translated from the Kannada by Srinath Perur

Hindutva or Hind Swaraj
U.R. Ananthamurthy
Translated from the Kannada by Keerti Ramachandra and Vivek Shanbhag

The Liberation of Sita
Volga
Translated from the Telugu by T. Vijay Kumar and C. Vijayasree

A Life Misspent
Suryakant Tripathi Nirala
Translated from the Hindi by Satti Khanna

The Sea Lies Ahead
Intizar Husain
Translated from the Urdu by Rakhshanda Jalil

Selected Poems
Joy Goswami
Translated from the Bengali by Sampurna Chattarji

Wild Animals Prohibited
Subimal Misra
Translated from the Bengali by V. Ramaswamy

Wild Words
Malathi Maithri, Salma, Kutti Revathi and Sukirtharani
Translated from the Tamil by Lakshmi Holmström

HarperCollins *Publishers* India

At HarperCollins India, we believe in telling the best stories and finding the widest readership for our books in every format possible. We started publishing in 1992; a great deal has changed since then, but what has remained constant is the passion with which our authors write their books, the love with which readers receive them, and the sheer joy and excitement that we as publishers feel in being a part of the publishing process.

Over the years, we've had the pleasure of publishing some of the finest writing from the subcontinent and around the world, including several award-winning titles and some of the biggest bestsellers in India's publishing history. But nothing has meant more to us than the fact that millions of people have read the books we published, and that somewhere, a book of ours might have made a difference.

As we look to the future, we go back to that one word—a word which has been a driving force for us all these years.

Read.

Harper Collins · 4th · HARPER PERENNIAL · HARPER BUSINESS · HARPER BLACK · हार्पर हिन्दी

HarperCollins *Children's Books* · HARPER DESIGN · HARPER VANTAGE · Harper Sport